An Analysis of

Maimonides's

The Guide
of the Perplexed

Mark W. Scarlata

Published by Macat International Ltd
24:13 Coda Centre, 189 Munster Road, London SW6 6AW.

Distributed exclusively by Routledge
2 Park Square, Milton Park, Abingdon, Oxon OX14 4RN
711 Third Avenue, New York, NY 10017, USA

Routledge is an imprint of the Taylor & Francis Group, an informa business

www.macat.com
info@macat.com

Cataloguing in Publication Data
A catalogue record for this book is available from the British Library.
Library of Congress Cataloguing-in-Publication Data is available upon request.
Cover illustration: Jonathan Edwards

ISBN 978-1-912453-81-8 (hardback)
ISBN 978-1-912453-63-4 (paperback)
ISBN 978-1-912453-69-6 (e-book)

Notice

CONTENTS

THE MACAT LIBRARY

The Macat Library is a series of unique academic explorations of seminal works in the humanities and social sciences – books and papers that have had a significant and widely recognised impact on their disciplines. It has been created to serve as much more than just a summary of what lies between the covers of a great book. It illuminates and explores the influences on, ideas of, and impact of that book. Our goal is to offer a learning resource that encourages critical thinking and fosters a better, deeper understanding of important ideas.

Each publication is divided into three Sections: Influences, Ideas, and Impact. Each Section has four Modules. These explore every important facet of the work, and the responses to it.

This Section-Module structure makes a Macat Library book easy to use, but it has another important feature. Because each Macat book is written to the same format, it is possible (and encouraged!) to cross-reference multiple Macat books along the same lines of inquiry or research. This allows the reader to open up interesting interdisciplinary pathways.

To further aid your reading, lists of glossary terms and people mentioned are included at the end of this book (these are indicated by an asterisk [*] throughout) – as well as a list of works cited.

Macat has worked with the University of Cambridge to identify the elements of critical thinking and understand the ways in which six different skills combine to enable effective thinking.
Three allow us to fully understand a problem; three more give us the tools to solve it. Together, these six skills make up the **PACIER** model of critical thinking. They are:

ANALYSIS – understanding how an argument is built
EVALUATION – exploring the strengths and weaknesses of an argument
INTERPRETATION – understanding issues of meaning

CREATIVE THINKING – coming up with new ideas and fresh connections
PROBLEM-SOLVING – producing strong solutions
REASONING – creating strong arguments

To find out more, visit **WWW.MACAT.COM.**

CRITICAL THINKING AND *THE GUIDE OF THE PERPLEXED*

Primary critical thinking skill: INTERPRETATION
Secondary critical thinking skill: REASONING

A key theme of Maimonides's work is using philosophical reasoning to help interpret the biblical texts that he examines. He engages with the work of philosophers such as Aristotle and Plato in order to harmonize philosophical concepts with how they are presented in the Hebrew Bible. It was critical for Maimonides to link the natural sciences and philosophy with the wisdom of his religious tradition, since he believed that all truth was from God.

One of the greatest medieval Jewish scholars, Maimonides excelled in philosophy, the natural sciences, and religious studies. His life was devoted to the interpretation of the biblical text in a way that both respected historical rabbinic writings and utilized classical Greek philosophy. Though many Jews disagreed with his approach, Maimonides insisted that to truly interpret and understand the Bible, one must approach the scripture with both reason and devotion.

Maimonides offers a key work of interpretation because he seeks a holistic approach to understanding biblical language and theological concepts. He aims to guide the reader along the path to wisdom and reason in an effort to establish a proper interpretation of the Bible. The goal of such interpretation is ultimately to know and experience God. In a medieval world often divided by religious tradition, Maimonides offered a new paradigm for biblical interpretation that embraced philosophy, the sciences, and traditional Jewish approaches to understanding God and revelation.

ABOUT THE AUTHOR OF THE ORIGINAL WORK

Moses ben Maimon, often called Maimonides, was born in Cordova, Spain, in 1135 and died in Cairo, Egypt, in 1204. At the age of 13, Maimonides and his family were forced from their home and led a semi-nomadic life for 12 years, wandering throughout Spain. In 1160, the family settled in Fez, Morocco, for about five years and then moved to Egypt, where Maimonides took up the practice of medicine. His writings include the *Mishneh Torah* (or *Repetition of Torah*), a 14-volume code of Jewish law; *The Guide of the Perplexed*; and other medical and scientific works.

ABOUT THE AUTHOR OF THE ANALYSIS

Mark Scarlata received an MA from Yale Divinity School and completed his doctoral dissertation at Cambridge University. He is currently lecturer in Old Testament Studies at St. Mellitus College, London. The Revd. Dr. Scarlata specializes in Hebrew Bible, ancient Near Eastern, and Judaic studies.

ABOUT MACAT

GREAT WORKS FOR CRITICAL THINKING

Macat is focused on making the ideas of the world's great thinkers accessible and comprehensible to everybody, everywhere, in ways that promote the development of enhanced critical thinking skills.

It works with leading academics from the world's top universities to produce new analyses that focus on the ideas and the impact of the most influential works ever written across a wide variety of academic disciplines. Each of the works that sit at the heart of its growing library is an enduring example of great thinking. But by setting them in context – and looking at the influences that shaped their authors, as well as the responses they provoked – Macat encourages readers to look at these classics and game-changers with fresh eyes. Readers learn to think, engage and challenge their ideas, rather than simply accepting them.

'Macat offers an amazing first-of-its-kind tool for interdisciplinary learning and research. Its focus on works that transformed their disciplines and its rigorous approach, drawing on the world's leading experts and educational institutions, opens up a world-class education to anyone.'

Andreas Schleicher
Director for Education and Skills, Organisation for Economic
Co-operation and Development

'Macat is taking on some of the major challenges in university education ... They have drawn together a strong team of active academics who are producing teaching materials that are novel in the breadth of their approach.'

Prof Lord Broers,
former Vice-Chancellor of the University of Cambridge

'The Macat vision is exceptionally exciting. It focuses upon new modes of learning which analyse and explain seminal texts which have profoundly influenced world thinking and so social and economic development. It promotes the kind of critical thinking which is essential for any society and economy. This is the learning of the future.'

Rt Hon Charles Clarke, former UK Secretary of State for Education

'The Macat analyses provide immediate access to the critical conversation surrounding the books that have shaped their respective discipline, which will make them an invaluable resource to all of those, students and teachers, working in the field.'

Professor William Tronzo, University of California at San Diego

WAYS IN TO THE TEXT

KEY POINTS

- Moses ben Maimon, called Maimonides, was a medieval Jewish* scholar who contributed to the integration of Jewish beliefs with traditional philosophy.

- *The Guide of the Perplexed* is a book written from Maimonides to his disciple in order to harmonize philosophical conceptions of God with the Bible.*

- *The Guide* is the most notable Jewish attempt to integrate the revelation of the Bible with traditional philosophical and scientific reasoning in the medieval world.

Who Was Maimonides?

Moses ben Maimon, often called Maimonides, was born in Cordova, Spain, in 1135 and died in Cairo, Egypt, in 1204. When he was 13, Maimonides and his family were compelled to choose between Islam* and exile when Cordova fell into the hands of the Muslim*Almohads.* He and his family chose the latter and for 12 years led a semi-nomadic life, wandering throughout Spain. In 1160, the family settled in Fez, Morocco, for about five years before moving to Egypt, where Maimonides took up the practice of medicine.[1]

Maimonides presumably received his rabbinical* instruction from his father, who was both a judge and a scholar of high degree. Maimonides lived at a time when Jewish intellectuals valued traditional Jewish study alongside secular scholarship; thus he was also schooled by Arabic masters in a full array of contemporary disciplines. Throughout his family's time of wandering in Spain, Maimonides continued his education alongside students of Islamic philosophers during the height of twelfth-century Aristotelian* study.

Before arriving in Egypt, Maimonides was exposed to the thriving intellectual climate of Andalusia in Muslim Spain. Under the reign of Caliph* 'Abd ar-Rahman III,* which lasted from 912 until 961, a policy of tolerance was adopted, and the region flourished with a diversity of religious and ethnic groups that were free to pursue secular learning in the arts, sciences, literature, and music.[2] For Jewish communities, the synthesis of traditional rabbinic learning and secular knowledge became the hallmark of the educated elite. It was in this environment that Maimonides excelled in his rabbinic and philosophical studies, giving him the reputation of being one of the great rabbis of his day.

What Does *The Guide* Say?

The core purpose of Maimonides's *The Guide of the Perplexed* was to explain difficult biblical terms for general readers. Another main inquiry—which occupies the first 49 chapters—relates to the nature of God's incorporeality* (i.e., that God does not exist in material form). God's existence and unity were fundamental truths in Judaism.* This belief was affirmed daily through the recitation of the *shema**: "Hear, O Israel, the Lord our God, the Lord is one" (Deuteronomy 6:4). The difficulty Maimonides addresses concerning God's incorporeality is that certain biblical texts suggest that God can be corporeal.* Maimonides argues that the risk of believing in God's corporeal nature is that it contradicts the belief that God is one.

The urgency Maimonides felt to establish God's incorporeality was caused by his desire to destroy any possible path that would lead to idolatry, which is the gravest sin and the greatest threat to life of a faithful Jew. If God is incorporeal, then he has no corporeal shape and cannot be worshipped through human-made images. He also argues against the Christian* understanding of the Trinity,* or the belief in God the Father, Son, and Holy Spirit, and condemned any idea of God's multiplicity.

The use of anthropomorphic* terms in the Bible and the question of God's nature had long been discussed in Jewish intellectual circles. Maimonides, however, separates himself from the mainstream by arguing for the unity of God through Aristotelian philosophy—this is despite the fact that he describes Aristotle as an idolater! Maimonides also relies on the works of the great philosopher to establish other universal principles relating to God's unity. He argues that heavenly bodies are superior to humanity and that creation is to be considered separate from the unity and incorporeality of God. He also discusses certain arguments for the existence of God, understanding the names of God, and issues relating to philosophical cosmology.* None of these questions were foreign to Jewish thinking, but Maimonides's method of using philosophical ideas to inform Scripture* was a significant departure from mainstream Jewish teaching.

In an age when the study of science and philosophy had become more commonplace among Jewish intellectuals, Maimonides felt the need to deal with the unresolved conflict between the religious teachings of the Bible and the non-religious truths of philosophy. *The Guide* was his attempt to resolve these perplexities and was born from Maimonides's desire to uncover and share the truth. The harmonization of religion with philosophy continues as an academic discipline today, and Maimonides's *Guide* offers one of the most significant Jewish attempts to integrate traditional philosophical principles with the revelation of the God of the Bible.

The Guide was not only influential on subsequent schools of Jewish thought; it was also a precursor to the great scholastic debates of medieval Christianity that wrestled with philosophical questions about God. Christians were drawn to Maimonides's arguments for a God who is firmly located in philosophical truth and who can enlighten the heart and intellect of humanity, leading them towards perfection. Maimonides's influence on Thomas Aquinas* is particularly noteworthy, but even modern theologians and philosophers have been shaped by the ideas and arguments in *The Guide.*

Why Does *The Guide* Matter?

Maimonides's *Guide* deserves our attention today because it is a conversation—in many ways a timeless one—between a master and his pupil that seeks to both reveal and conceal glimpses of universal truth. Maimonides did not set out to reconcile two distinct bodies of truth in *The Guide*—the scientific truths found in the cosmos and the truths of the Bible. Rather, he taught that faith and reason were unified and that the pursuit of truth involves a single path.

Yet rather than speaking plainly on any particular subject, *The Guide* still challenges contemporary thinkers since it is written in a genre that is, at times, esoteric and contains biblical exegesis,* philological analysis, philosophical reasoning, scientific proofs, and parable. As Maimonides himself struggles with unresolved and traditional questions about science, faith, and the end goal of humankind, he invites any reader—past or present—to wrestle with these questions as well.

In a postmodern age, Maimonides's claim to universal truth will undoubtedly face sharp criticism. Yet this need not discourage the modern student from reading *The Guide* because it still raises questions where decisive resolutions remain impossible. *The Guide* offers an invaluable dialogue that will lead any student down the path of religious and philosophical debates that continue today. Though particular arguments may have been surpassed by contemporary philosophy and theology, Maimonides' wisdom and clarity remain relevant for those pursuing matters of truth.

NOTES

1   D. Yellin and I. Abrahams, *Maimonides* (Skokie, IL: Varda Books, 2002), 33-54.

2   Joel L. Kraemer, *Maimonides: The Life and World of One of Civilization's Greatest Minds* (New York: Doubleday Press, 2008), 42-61.

SECTION 1
INFLUENCES

MODULE 1
THE AUTHOR AND THE HISTORICAL CONTEXT

KEY POINTS

- *The Guide of the Perplexed* contains a variety of genres and seeks to reconcile the Bible with contemporary science and philosophy.
- Maimonides grew up in a rich intellectual environment in Spain before fleeing to northern Egypt.
- Maimonides's exposure to Plato,* Aristotle,* and Islamic philosophers shaped his understanding and approach to the study of Jewish rabbis and the Bible.

Why Read This Text?

The main purpose of Maimonides's *The Guide of the Perplexed* was to remove the perplexities of the Bible for those who read it in the light of philosophical truths. His hope was to enable the intellectually sophisticated reader to understand any apparent inconsistencies in the biblical text and to help them discover its hidden meanings. He does not do this, however, in a clear, systematic way. Instead, he informs the reader that his work—like the Bible—is filled with secret meanings that can only be grasped by those who are philosophically astute.

The work contains a variety of genres, from biblical exegesis, philosophical reasoning, and scientific inquiry to parable, narrative, and dialogue. Though *The Guide* covers a variety of philosophical topics, Maimonides uses the language of Scripture* as his starting point in each instance.

The Guide was composed during an intellectually stimulating period in Egypt, when there was much philosophical and scientific

> **❝** Thus Maimonides was already preparing himself to take the lead in medieval scholasticism and to found a philosophy of religion on a basis, at first unconsciously, yet in the end essentially, constructed on a syncretism between Greek metaphysics and Hebrew revelation. **❞**
>
> David Yellin and Israel Abrahams, *Maimonides*

interest.[1] Stylistically, *The Guide* is dialogical, and, like Plato, Maimonides sought to teach by allusion rather than to impart authoritative knowledge. His desire was to uphold philosophical truths in relation to the biblical texts without disrupting social norms or discouraging faithful religious belief. With a heavy emphasis on philosophy and science, Maimonides wrote *The Guide* to instruct others along the path of both perfect reason *and* biblical wisdom, so that they might become fully human and delight in a passionate love for God.

Author's Life

Maimonides was born and raised in southern Spain during a turbulent time between Christian and Muslim rule. The Spanish Aristotelians were possibly the most significant intellectual influence he received in Andalusia. These philosophers were not only disciples of Aristotle but were also influenced by Neoplatonic* thought. Averroës,* a contemporary of Maimonides, was a devout disciple of Aristotle and a particularly influential thinker. Though we do not have any record of the two scholars meeting, later in life (presumably after he wrote *The Guide*), Maimonides read some of Averroës's work on Aristotle and strongly recommended it to his friends.

With the rise of Muslim Almohad oppression in the twelfth century, the intellectual and political freedom Maimonides enjoyed under the caliph came to an end, and he was forced into exile, where he continued his studies. Despite their religious intolerance, the Almohads did advance the study of the sciences and philosophy. One scholar who might have influenced Maimonides from this period was Ibn Tumart,* who contended that one could not ascribe positive attributes to the divine. His ideas were based on the writings of the Muslim theologian al-Ghazali* and possibly contributed to Maimonides's vigorous condemnation of anthropomorphism* in *The Guide*.[2]

After he arrived in Egypt, Maimonides came under the support of a patron named Al-Qādī al-Fādil al-Baysani* (1135–1200), a scholar who had amassed a collection of Arabic works. Under al-Baysani, Maimonides rose to become the highest judicial authority among the Jews and benefited from an open and tolerant atmosphere under the caliph. It is likely that during this time he had access to Ismāʿīlī* writings and lectures, which may also have influenced his theory of negative predication, or the belief that God could only be spoken of in terms of what he is not, rather than what he is (a stance known as apophatic theology*).[3]

Author's Background

It is probable that Maimonides received much of his early education from his father, but there is no actual evidence that this was the case. For one so well read in philosophy, very little is known about his teachers. Maimonides does mention some of his instructors in the context of astronomy, but he does not cite any regarding philosophy. Some scholars have concluded that he was self-taught.

In the twelfth-century Islamic* cultures of Spain, Morocco, and Egypt, Maimonides was surrounded by a rich intellectual tradition of Christian and Muslim theology as well as ancient secular philosophy. Works by Plato, Aristotle, and other ancient philosophers had been translated into Arabic and had a significant influence on Maimonides. In *The Guide*, Aristotle is most frequently cited, and we know through comments found in Maimonides's other letters that he held the ancient philosopher in the highest regard. He unquestionably accepted the supremacy of Aristotle and relied on his writings for all matters referring to logic, physics, and metaphysics. As far as we know, there is no reason to doubt that Maimonides had access to the whole corpus of Aristotle's writings except, possibly, for *Politics*.

NOTES

1   Sarah Stroumsa, *Maimonides in His World: Portrait of a Mediterranean Thinker*, (Princeton, NJ: Princeton University Press, 2009), 1-21.

2   D. Yellin and I. Abrahams, *Maimonides*, (Skokie, IL: Varda Books, 2002), 1-16.

3   Joel Kraemer, "Moses Maimonides: An Intellectual Portrait," In *The Cambridge Companion to Maimonides,* ed. K. Seeskin (Cambridge: Cambridge University Press, 2005), 10-18.

ACADEMIC CONTEXT

KEY POINTS

- Maimonides wrote *The Guide of the Perplexed* during a time of great scientific and philosophical inquiry in Christian, Islamic, and Jewish thought.
- *The Guide* offers a philosophical and scientific approach to the study of the Bible in a field that was influenced by Plato and Aristotle.
- Maimonides was shaped by some of the great Islamic thinkers of his period and sought to balance Aristotelian philosophy with biblical revelation.

The Work In Its Context

Maimonides was the pre-eminent champion of Jewish rationalism, and *The Guide of the Perplexed* can be seen as one of the most significant examples of medieval Jewish philosophy. He met the needs of a Jewish culture that cherished secular learning through science and ancient philosophy, yet also held firmly to religious tradition. As a faithful Jew, Maimonides was convinced that no philosophic theory could provide a rational account of the universe as a whole. And, despite the seeming contradictions and mysteries contained in the biblical texts, he argued that Scripture provided the necessary instruction to lead one in the paths of life.

At a time of great philosophical and scientific inquiry in Latin Christian, Islamic, and Jewish thought, Maimonides sought to deliver the reader from superstitious beliefs, or idolatrous practices, and bring them to the goal of intellectual peace and spiritual transformation. He wrote to a growing class of educated Jews and scholars who were

> ❝ As Maimonides is communicating oral discourse in writing, the reader of the *Guide* should not expect anything beyond intimations, and these are dispersed among other subjects. The message of the *Guide* is scattered throughout its chapters, and the reader must pick up hints and join them to form a coherent account. ❞
>
> Joel Kraemer, "Moses Maimonides: An Intellectual Portrait" in *The Cambridge Companion to Maimonides*

troubled by the philosophical and textual inconsistencies of the Bible. Yet rather than concede to the secular thought of his day, Maimonides addressed both cognitive and spiritual issues in order to alleviate any irrational fears and anxieties that an educated person might experience in the study of Scripture.

Maimonides made no claim that *The Guide* would provide specific answers, but he held to the view that humans could only understand imperfectly. He argued that reason had its limits and that, despite the benefits of scientific knowledge, there were matters that were beyond the capabilities of the human intellect. In some ways, *The Guide* is a timeless work that addresses the potential obstacles that can exist between science, reason, and religious faith. In an effort to bridge these gaps, *The Guide* offers a reasoned account of Scripture that draws on Aristotle and other philosophers and that not only suited the intelligentsia of Maimonides's day, but also provided a foundation of biblical and philosophical inquiry for generations to come.

Overview Of The Field
Surrounded by the philosophical and scientific works of Islamic scholars such as Avicenna* and Averroës, Maimonides was shaped by an intellectual climate that privileged reason and rational thinking.

Within this context, Maimonides was eager to bring his own Jewish religious tradition in line with contemporary thinking.[1] He deeply valued the revelation of God proclaimed in the Bible, but he was also aware that the language of the Bible often contradicted philosophical principles. In an effort to bring his tradition into dialogue with the intellectual movement of his day, Maimonides set out to integrate biblical truth with philosophical truth.

Not everyone, however, was convinced of *The Guide*'s ability to harmonize philosophy and the sciences with biblical texts. Many rabbinic leaders saw Maimonides's work as an attack on Jewish belief. One significant issue was *The Guide*'s attempt to move away from the anthropomorphic language of the Bible in favor of a more nuanced, philosophical understanding. This type of allegorical reading stood in contrast to the more established literal readings of the Bible. Other critics, such as the Ashkenazi* Jews from northern France, argued that *The Guide* replaced traditional rabbinic teaching with secular philosophy, which threatened the foundations of Judaism. Despite these protests, however, *The Guide* was welcomed by many as a refreshing perspective on how to live faithfully by one's religious convictions without sacrificing reason and intellect.

Academic Influences

Some of Maimonides's philosophical influences were made known through a letter to his translator, Samuel Ibn Tibbon.*[2] He wrote that he dismissed Plato's work largely because it was written in parables that were difficult to understand. However, he considered Aristotle to represent the pinnacle of human intellect and provide the foundations for all works in the sciences. He also relied on the commentaries of Alexander of Aphrodisias,* Themistius,* Avicenna, and Averroës. Alexander is quoted several times in *The Guide*, and the Spanish Aristotelians held his commentaries in high regard. Some scholars suggest that Maimonides was influenced by the Ismā'īlī and

Neoplatonic doctrines he was exposed to in Egypt. It is likely, however, that he had already been acquainted with this literature in Andalusia.

Unlike the competing *kalām** theology of his day, Maimonides held strictly to philosophical inquiry and largely shunned some of the prevailing trends in mysticism.[3] He extolled men like the ninth-century Muslim philosopher and scientist al- Fārābī,* whose works are mentioned throughout *The Guide* on topics such as logic, *kalām*, and the nature of providence. He also spoke highly of Abū Bakr Ibn Bājja* (also called Avempace) and cites him in *The Guide* on topics regarding the intellect and the challenges that astronomy posed to Aristotle's metaphysics.

Despite his love for philosophy, Maimonides was also a faithful Jew and a devout student of rabbinic interpretation, which also shaped his thinking. He was committed to God's law as revealed through Scripture, and although he regarded Aristotle as "the Chief of the Philosophers," he spoke of Moses* as the "master of those who know."[4] When we approach *The Guide*, therefore, we find Maimonides effortlessly weaving Aristotelian metaphysics and rabbinic tradition as he presents his interpretation of the biblical texts.

NOTES

1   Sarah Stroumsa, *Maimonides in His World: Portrait of a Mediterranean Thinker*, (Princeton, NJ: Princeton University Press, 2009), 24-52.

2   Alexander Marx, "Texts by and About Maimonides," *Jewish Quarterly Review*, N.S. 25 (1934): 374–81.

3   Stroumsa, *Maimonides in His World, 26-38.*

4   Maimonides, *The Guide of the Perplexed*, ed. Shlomo Pines (Chicago: University of Chicago Press, 1960), 1:54.

MODULE 3
THE PROBLEM

KEY POINTS

- Maimonides sought to answer the question of how ancient Jewish religious traditions could be aligned with philosophical thought.

- A wide range of Islamic philosophers influenced Maimonides's approach to theological problems of revelation and God's governing of the world.

- Maimonides presents a synthesis of religious and philosophical traditions that offer examples of how religion and reason work together.

Core Question

In his introduction, Maimonides describes the *The Guide of the Perplexed* as "a key permitting one to enter places, the gates to which were locked. When those gates are opened and those places are entered, the souls will find rest therein, the eyes will be delighted, and the bodies will be eased of their toil and of their labor."[1] The core question he sets out to answer is how one can understand the wisdom of the Jewish tradition in relation to the great philosophical traditions of the West. His intent is to explain specific biblical terms that might cause difficulty for the educated reader and to open up the truths found in the biblical text. In the light of philosophical and scientific reasoning, Maimonides tries to merge rabbinic tradition and biblical interpretation with an intellectual reasoning that resonates with the scholasticism of his day.

The Guide can be seen as both a book of philosophy and a Jewish book. Maimonides relies on reason and rationality as a philosopher, but

> **❝** Maimonides wants to raise the reader from imaginary and superstitious beliefs that cause fear to a rational consciousness that brings equanimity. The reward is a new vision of the world, intellectual serenity, self-transformation, and spiritual conversion. The aim of the *Guide* is to enlighten and to give peace and tranquility to body and soul. **❞**
>
> Joel Kraemer, "Moses Maimonides: An Intellectual Portrait" in *The Cambridge Companion to Maimonides*

he takes the acceptance of the truth of Scripture as his starting point. Thus he intends to explain the Bible's meaning by taking into account both its plain sense and its hidden, or inner, meaning. Maimonides writes that he is devoted to revealing the "difficulties of the law" and the "secrets of the law."[2] *The Guide* is therefore intended for a public audience in its general teaching as well as a select audience whose members have the wisdom to comprehend Scripture's secret teaching.

The Participants

Maimonides engaged with Jewish rabbinic tradition and Islamic thinkers. It is likely that his naturalistic views on prophecy were influenced by al-Fārābī, who emphasized the political role of the prophet and argued that revelation is consistent with philosophy. If revelation is conditional on intellectual perfection, then human beings have a significant role in prophetic activity. Maimonides, however, parts ways with al-Fārābī in his understanding of the uniqueness of Moses's revelation and his ability to legislate divine law.[3] What is most striking about Maimonides's writings on prophetic activity is that they do not stipulate that prophets need be of Jewish descent. This stands in opposition to the fourteenth century Jewish philosopher Crescas,* who contended that prophecy was reserved for Jews alone.

Many of Maimonides's arguments are intimately connected to Aristotelian philosophy, especially regarding the problem of evil. In spite of numerous objections, Maimonides upholds the notion of God's omniscience and the fact that his divine knowledge does not impinge upon his unchanging essence. This view did not go unchallenged, and Gersonides* (1288–1344) attempted to modify Maimonides's views by stating that God does not have foreknowledge of particular future contingents, but rather knowledge of how things *might* happen. In other words, God knows all the general possibilities for future existing states, but he does not know which of these alternatives will be realized. Thus, Gersonides argued for a "general providence" that governs the universe, and a "special providence" that pertains to the individual.[4] Whereas Maimonides argued for the complete otherness of God, Gersonides contended that God still plays a role in relation to those who strive for spiritual perfection and thereby preserves human freedom and responsibility.

The Contemporary Debate

Maimonides has been simultaneously praised and criticized for his philosophical approach to the Bible. Possibly the most controversial stance he takes within the Jewish religion is the priority he gives to the intellect—especially in relation to prophecy—over traditional study of the law. Rather than relying on moral virtue or obedience to Scripture, Maimonides emphasizes philosophical contemplation as a means to knowing the divine. This stood in contrast to centuries of rabbinic thought.

Though *The Guide* might not have much direct influence outside its field of study and in contemporary debate, the rational teachings of Maimonides continue to have relevance today as an example of how reason relates to religious faith and how the two need not be separated.

When we examine Maimonides's writings in *The Guide*, we discover a Western scientific and philosophical foundation in logic, mathematics, and medicine, combined with the moral, legal, and spiritual values of the Jewish tradition. A large part of Maimonides's appeal to contemporary fields in academia (especially theology) is based on his ability to engage with a broad spectrum of scholarship, whether it was ancient Greek thinkers or contemporary Muslim philosophers or scientists. His intellectual breadth and openness make *The Guide* a lasting model of creative synthesis that can be applied across academic disciplines.

NOTES

1   Maimonides, *The Guide of the Perplexed,* ed. Shlomo Pines (Chicago: University of Chicago Press, 1960), Introduction, 12a.

2   Maimonides, *The Guide*, xiv.

3   Maimonides, *The Guide*, xxviii-xcii.

4   Tamar Rudavsky, *Maimonides* (Oxford: Wiley-Blackwell, 2010), 157.

MODULE 4
THE AUTHOR'S CONTRIBUTION

KEY POINTS

- Maimonides aimed to defend the incorporeality of God through a conversational model that revealed the hidden wisdom of the Bible.

- Maimonides approached Jewish teachings with an engaging blend of philosophy and traditional rabbinic interpretation.

- *The Guide* offered the most comprehensive and coherent syntheses of Jewish law, biblical interpretation, and philosophy of Maimonides's time.

Author's Aims

Maimonides's *The Guide of the Perplexed* was a defense of the unity and incorporeality of the God of the Hebrew Bible. This grew out of his extensive education in the natural sciences and Greek and Islamic philosophy. A similar synthesis of Jewish and philosophical materials can be traced throughout his writings and is not particular to *The Guide*. The main difference we see in *The Guide*, however, is the lack of systematic exposition that is demonstrated in his earlier work, the *Mishneh Torah*. Instead, Maimonides choses a dialogical style that employs allusion and conversation as a means of discovering truth. It is possible that, at an older age, or perhaps because of the topic, Maimonides preferred a style that was less straightforward and more mystical in nature. With access to the philosophical traditions that were then commonly used in the educational curriculum, many would have been familiar with the references in *The Guide* and might have had less difficulty interpreting its meaning.

> 66 Strauss suggests that the *Guide* seems to have been closer to a conversation between friends, and as such, this 'book' should be read almost as one would approach a Platonic dialogue: in terms of characters, setting, historical situation, dramatic plot, type of work (comedy, tragedy, etc.), theme, etc. 99
>
> Kenneth Green, *Leo Strauss and the Rediscovery of Maimonides*

In an intellectual climate in which Jewish and Islamic philosophical contemporaries debated over the classic tension between faith and reason, Maimonides entered into the discussion by offering a single path that uses both Scripture and philosophy. He proposed a method of biblical exegesis that allows the reader to move beyond the literal meaning of Scripture in order to comprehend "flashes" of its truth. For those who were steeped in biblical and philosophical study, the danger of existential perplexity was an ever-present reality. Maimonides attempted to alleviate this confusion in *The Guide* in order to lead people to the truth.[1]

Approach

The Guide is intended primarily for Jews who are familiar with the sciences and philosophy, yet who remain perplexed by the literal meaning of Jewish law. The work is dedicated to his disciple Joseph ben Judah,* who had studied under him for some time. Judah appears to have been interested in learning about divine things but had not yet mastered the natural sciences. Throughout *The Guide*, therefore, Maimonides supplies his readers with a basic grounding in this area. At 1:26, for example, he writes, "It has been demonstrated that everything moved undoubtedly possesses a magnitude and is divisible; and it will be demonstrated that God possesses no magnitude and hence possesses no motion."[2] What Maimonides has "demonstrated" here is that he presupposes a knowledge, and acceptance, of Aristotle's principle of motion in *Physics*. Maimonides assumed the role of expert in the natural sciences so that he might reveal that which belongs to divine science. According to his method, his audience must be satisfied with his suppositions before agreeing to his theological conclusions.

Maimonides chose this style of teaching because he believed that the natural sciences had the potential to corrupt any person who was not perfect in obedience to the Scripture.[3] In an effort not to upset people with the potential dangers of the natural sciences, he proceeds in a manner that appeals to the weaker believers and writes as a more conservative Jew. Maimonides believed strongly that moral perfection must come before intellectual mastery; thus, he often encourages his readers to acquire the habits of doing noble deeds and practicing temperance in their intellectual pursuits.

Contribution In Context

The contributions of *The Guide* were not necessarily unique to Maimonides. Contemporary Jewish and Islamic philosophers were also wrestling with theological and philosophical questions regarding the nature of God, creation, the order of the universe and the language we use to speak about these things. What is significant about *The Guide* is that it represents one of the most comprehensive and coherent syntheses of Jewish law, biblical interpretation, and philosophy. No one during Maimonides's lifetime had achieved such a unification of ancient Jewish religious tradition with contemporary scientific and rational thought.

The Guide is also distinctive in the way that it presents these interconnected strands of truth. Instead of systematic exposition, Maimonides offers the wisdom of a teacher imparting knowledge to a student in a work that contains various levels of meaning. He warns his reader in the introduction that his work will contain simple, outward meanings as well as hidden, esoteric truths. Scholars have debated what the esoteric truths are, but whether the secrets lie in the spheres of metaphysics and the sciences or Scripture and morality, they will only be revealed to the enlightened thinker. Thus, as a tool for communicating ideas, *The Guide* is both lucid and obscure at the same time.

NOTES

1   Herbert A. Davidson, *Moses Maimonides: The Man and his Works* (Oxford: Oxford University Press, 2005), 538-42.

2   Maimonides, *The Guide of the Perplexed,* .ed. Shlomo Pines (Chicago: University of Chicago Press, 1960), 1:26.

3   Maimonides, *Guide,* 1:62.

SECTION 2
IDEAS

MODULE 5
MAIN IDEAS

KEY POINTS

- Maimonides focuses on what we can know about God, the structure and existence of the universe, and how Biblical images of God might be reconciled with philosophy.

- He was concerned with linguistic accuracy when speaking about God and how we can come to know God.

- The fragmentary and dialogical nature of *The Guide* contribute to Maimonides's conviction that one cannot speak directly about Scripture.

Key Themes

Maimonides's *The Guide of the Perplexed* is primarily concerned with a philosophical and theological understanding of God as revealed through Scripture and in the light of human reason. The work is divided into three parts, or books, and the beginning of the first book deals chiefly with conceptions of the divine and the question of how anthropomorphic attributes given to God should be understood.[1] Maimonides analyzes the Hebrew words used to describe God, defines their meaning, and then examines the words in the context of philosophical truth. He concludes that many terms must be understood allegorically and that, ultimately, one can only speak of the divine using negative language, a stance known as apophatic theology. Following these initial 50 chapters, Maimonides touches briefly on the divine names for God, his essence, and how God relates to the world. The first book concludes with a detailed critique of the arguments put forward by the Mutakallimūn* regarding the nature of God and his incorporeality.

> ❝ In Maimonides' judgment, Judaism stands or falls on its commitment to an incorporeal God who cannot be represented in bodily form. ❞
>
> Kenneth Seeskin, introduction to *The Cambridge Companion to Maimonides*

The second book of *The Guide* begins with Maimonides's view on the nature and existence of God. He then turns to an exposition of the structure of the universe, and much of his reasoning is based on Aristotelian cosmology. He discusses the organization of the heavenly spheres, drawing on Aristotle's notion of God as the "prime mover." Maimonides then addresses the creation account in Genesis, and, by explaining its language and allegorical terms, he harmonizes the biblical narrative with philosophical thought by arguing that God is the creator of the heavenly spheres and that from him they derived their motion. The next section is a discussion of biblical prophecy, in which Maimonides outlines several levels of prophetic activity and the nature of the prophetic books of the Bible.

The third book begins with an exposition on the narrative of the chariot revealed to the prophet Ezekiel,* which was a sensitive text in Jewish interpretation because of its mystical nature and its anthropomorphic depiction of God. Following this is a discussion of theodicy* or the problem of evil and divine providence. Maimonides argues that evil cannot come from God since it has no positive existence, explaining that when Scripture speaks of God sending evil upon someone, this must be interpreted allegorically. In the final section, he discusses the 613 laws contained in the five books of Moses, also called the Torah,* and concludes with a depiction of the perfect and happy life that is founded on the correct worship of God.

Exploring The Ideas

Since *The Guide* was written for the educated Jewish reader, Maimonides devotes a significant portion of his work to biblical language that suggests God's physical nature. In the first book, he continually reminds his reader that language is a human construct and must, therefore, be deconstructed in order to be understood correctly when speaking about God. Maimonides argues that any anthropomorphism must be interpreted based on God's incorporeal nature. Thus when God "speaks" or "comes down," it must be viewed allegorically, because God cannot have a physical mouth or body.[2] This type of deconstruction was groundbreaking for contemporary Jewish interpretation and stood in antithesis to traditional rabbinic teaching.

Linguistic accuracy was critical for Maimonides, who argued that "belief is not the notion that is uttered, but the notion that is represented in the soul when it has been averred of it that it is in fact just as it has been represented."[3] In this view, improper belief means believing something that is different from what that thing really is.[4] Maimonides thus sets out to break down anthropomorphic and corporeal conceptions about God and replaces them with a philosophical foundation based on God's incorporeality and unity. He contends that if one continues to believe that God has a physical form, one is in danger of committing idolatry.[5]

Another critical debate during Maimonides's time concerned cosmogony,* or how the existence or beginning of the world should be understood; cosmology,* or what the world is composed of; and epistemology,* or how one can *know* about the world. One particular theory of creation that he rejected came from the Islamic *kalām* theologians.[6] The premise of the *kalām* argument was that the universe was composed of atoms that, when combined, form bodies. These individual particles act under the cause, or will, of God, and so there is no necessary link between cause and effect, but only God's will. In this view, God can create, shape, and form particles in any way he wants, demonstrating his omnipotence. Without going into great detail on *kalām* atomism, Maimonides rejects some of its proposals on the grounds of basic geometry.[7] Other arguments he simply dismisses as "abhorrent" and concludes that the principles of *kalām* atomism "are derived from premises that run counter to the nature of existence that is perceived."[8] In other words, they do not accord with Aristotle's theories regarding the cause and effect and motion of the heavenly bodies, or with those regarding their eternal existence.

Language And Expression

All of these themes, however, are not systematically organized in *The Guide*. Rather, *The Guide* is a collection of fragmentary ideas in which lessons are often taught by way of allusion and through hints rather than direct propositions. Maimonides defends this style by contending that explicit discourse on the parables of Scripture would be inappropriate and would not do justice to their truth. Despite the disjointed nature of *The Guide*, Maimonides successfully engages philosophical reasoning to mount a coherent defense of the existence of God and his incorporeal nature.

One way that Maimonides tries to enrich the reader's understanding is by allegorizing the literal meanings of Scripture in order to clarify God's incorporeality. For example, in Genesis 1:26-27, God creates human beings and declares that he has made them after his own "image and likeness." In response to this, Maimonides contends that the term "image" does not refer to the identical visible shape but rather to the specific form or the essence of God's being. Being created in the image of God therefore means that humans are endowed with divine intellect and have been gifted the ability to think and reason. Such biblical exegesis was a significant departure from traditional rabbinic interpretation, but it allowed students of philosophy to harmonize the biblical text with philosophical thought.

Though Maimonides's instruction is at times obscure, his lucid thinking and articulate arguments offered contemporary educated readers a foundation for belief in the truth of Scripture amidst the philosophic and scientific discourse of the day.

NOTES

1   Aryeh Tepper. *Progressive Minds, Conservative Politics: Leo Strauss's Later Writings on Maimonides*. (Albany: State University of New York Press, 2013), 23-39.

2   Maimonides, *The Guide of the Perplexed,* ed. Shlomo Pines (Chicago: University of Chicago Press, 1960), 1:65.

3   Maimonides, *Guide*, 1:50.

4   Maimonides, *Guide,* 1:36.

5   Maimonides, *Guide*, 1:36.

6   Maimonides, *Guide*, 1:71–6.

7   Maimonides, *Guide*, 1:73.

8   Maimonides, *Guide*, 1:71.

MODULE 6
SECONDARY IDEAS

KEY POINTS

- Prophecy and prophets also play a key role in *The Guide of the Perplexed* along with theories of creation and God's role in the universe.

- Intellectual perfection was central to Maimonides's understanding of human knowledge and experience of God.

- Maimonides is unclear about the end goal of humanity's happiness and whether it comes through intellectual perfection or by action in the world.

Other Ideas

The key ideas in Maimonides's *The Guide of the Perplexed* focus on the language of Scripture, the nature of God, and the doctrine of creation, but Maimonides also addressed other significant topics such as prophecy, the problem of evil, and the key to a happy life.

In his introduction to the text, Maimonides speaks of the prophetic parables as "apples of gold in settings of silver."[1] He argues that prophetic communication speaks on different levels and that the esoteric statements of the prophets convey truth for the masses as well as wisdom for those who can see beyond their surface meaning. He also argues that there are two types of prophetic parable: one in which each word can carry different meanings, and another in which a word expresses a single meaning.

Maimonides also wrestled with the doctrine that God is unified, unchanging, all-powerful, and all-knowing, which challenged his belief that God is involved with a changing world and that the divine

> ❝ [So] it behooves that they should be made to accept on traditional authority the belief that God is not a body; and that there is absolutely no likeness in any respect whatever between Him and the things created by Him. ❞
>
> Maimonides, *The Guide of the Perplexed*, 1:35

will acts within history. Indeed, although Maimonides held that God is omniscient and knows all past and future events, he responds to concerns about the problem of evil and divine goodness by arguing that the term "knowledge" is ambiguous and cannot be defined precisely when referring to God and human beings. Ultimately, Maimonides's position leaves the reader with unresolved questions about God's responsibility for human suffering and about human free will.

Other secondary teachings can be found in Maimonides's theory of creation. Some of his followers, such as Samuel ibn Tibbon, argued that the secret knowledge of creation revealed in *The Guide* was the view that Moses and Aristotle put forth the same truth about the universe and stand on equal ground.

Exploring The Ideas

Prophecy and the character of the prophet were important issues for Maimonides. In *The Guide*, he argues that God speaks only through those with proper intellectual perfection and that he may still withhold revelation even from those who satisfy the requisites for being a prophet. This naturalistic view of prophecy enabled Maimonides to justify the pursuit of philosophical knowledge, since one could only receive the divine word after achieving intellectual perfection.[2] Yet this also raises the question as to whether anyone, either Jew or gentile,* is able to act as a prophet. Diverging from traditional Jewish teaching,

Maimonides believed that everyone is equally born with the capacity to perfect his or her intellect and can, theoretically, receive a prophecy from God.

Among the various themes of *The Guide* is the end goal of for human knowledge and experience of God. How can God be known? Maimonides answers this question in the form of a parable[3] about a king's palace which describes the state of those who live in a particular kingdom. Whereas some of the subjects live outside the city with no intention of going in, others seek the palace, but never actually enter. Still others make their way into the outer courts, while some access the innermost parts of the palace. In summary, Maimonides encourages his students to be like those who enter the inner places of the palace: that is, those who perfect their study of philosophy and the natural sciences as well as their study of the Scriptures. Maimonides concludes by stating four pathways to perfection: material goods, bodily health, moral action, and contemplation of divine matters.

Overlooked

The Guide of the Perplexed has been thoroughly examined by both Jewish and secular scholars since its composition, and there are few areas that have not been commented on in depth. One area, however, that can be further explored is Maimonides's claims about the end goal of human existence. Maimonides argued that knowledge alone could lead to human immortality and that people should strive for intellectual perfection. The difficulty with this position is that Maimonides has already argued that human beings have a finite capacity for knowledge as well as corporeal limitations. He also contradicts traditional rabbinic teaching that emphasizes obedience to the law rather than intellectual achievements. The esoteric nature of humanity's end goal in *The Guide* leaves Maimonides's whole work open to interpretation.

Maimonides's cryptic parable of the king's palace,[4] his argument that only three people ultimately achieved perfection (Moses, Aaron, and Miriam), and his doctrine of the four perfections seem to express his belief in at least the possibility of intellectual perfection. His most direct discussion of perfection comes at the end of Chapter 51, where Maimonides describes the ultimate bliss of human achievement. He goes on to describe the path to the final goal of intellectual contemplation of God, instructs his pupil to "Take great care during these precious times not to set your thought to work on anything other than intellectual worship consisting in nearness to God and being in his presence in that true reality that I have made known to you, and not by way of affections of the imagination."[5]

Following this, however, Maimonides sets out his model of four perfections, but concludes with a fifth pathway: the imitation of God. He argues that as we come to a more perfect knowledge of the glory of God, our actions will be dictated by divine acts of loving kindness, judgment, and righteousness. Scholars have debated how to interpret this final point as the climax of human existence. Does this represent a life of action over contemplation? Some have argued that Maimonides contradicts his former arguments by advocating a life of practical activity rather than intellectual perfection.[6] Others, however, contend that practical activity for Maimonides was the inevitable result of the intellectual life.[7]

NOTES

1   Maimonides, *The Guide of the Perplexed,* ed. Shlomo Pines (Chicago: University of Chicago Press, 1960), Introduction, 6b.

2   For further discussion, see Charles H. Manekin, "Divine Will in Maimonides's Later Writings," in *Maimonidean Studies*, ed. A. Hyman and A. Ivry (New Jersey: Ktav, 2008), 189–222.

3   Maimonides, *Guide,* 3:51.

4   Maimonides, *Guide,* 3:51.

5   Maimonides, *Guide,* 3:51.

6   See Shlomo Pines, "The Limitations of Knowledge According to Al-Farabi, Ibn Bajja, and Maimonides," in *Studies in Medieval Jewish History and Literature*, ed. I. Twersky (Cambridge, MA: Harvard University Press, 1979), 82–109.

7   David Shatz, "Maimonides's Moral Theory," in *The Cambridge Companion to Maimonides*, ed. K. Seeskin (Cambridge: Cambridge University Press, 2005), 167–93.

MODULE 7
ACHIEVEMENT

KEY POINTS

- *The Guide of the Perplexed* was successful in what it set out to achieve by providing a work that integrated philosophy, science, and religious tradition.

- Maimonides's *Guide* had a wide influence in the medieval world and was embraced by Jewish, Christian, and Islamic thinkers.

- *The Guide* continues to be relevant as a classic work of religious and philosophical thought that engages with issues relevant to humanity today.

Assessing The Argument

Maimonides's *The Guide of the Perplexed* introduced fresh thinking into Jewish theology and philosophy. His attempt to harmonize the God of the Bible with philosophical truth was successful in that it left a lasting influence on Judaism as well as other religions. In an effort to elevate reason when addressing the perplexities found in Scripture, Maimonides raised more questions than he provided answers, which is one of the most important contributions of *The Guide*. This encouraged generations of Jewish, Christian, and Muslim thinkers to refute, embrace, and build upon his work in an effort to reconcile philosophical and scientific study with religious tradition.

The Guide proved to be a great beacon for other Jewish scholars because of its intellectual force and Maimonides's commitment to Jewish law. He opened the door to a religious life that could satisfy both intellectual rigor and moral truth, which he believed would lead to the goodness and perfection of humanity. The culmination of *The*

> ❝To the extent that the quantity of scholarly studies about an author is a criterion for either importance or fame, Moses Maimonides (1138 – 1204) stands among the most prominent figures in Jewish history, and certainly the most famous medieval Jewish thinker.❞
>
> Sarah Stroumsa, *Maimonides in His World: Portrait of a Mediterranean Thinker*

Guide embodies this concept of religious faith, and since its publication, nearly all philosophical developments in Judaism have taken Maimonides and his *Guide* as their starting point.

Not long after *The Guide's* publication, Muslim philosophers began citing it in their works, other Muslim authors wrote commentaries on portions of it, and the Muslim historian al-Qifti* wrote that *The Guide* represented the most significant work of his age.[1] Like other great philosophers—whether Islamic, Christian, or Greek—Maimonides's works transcend traditional religious parameters, and his commitment to free inquiry and high standards continues to appeal to a wide and diverse audience.

Achievement In Context

A history of Islamic or Christian philosophy is rarely composed without some reference to Maimonides. While it may not always be possible to point to specific people who have been influenced by his work, *The Guide* is a text that lies at the heart of medieval Western thought and that has had a profound impact on theologians, philosophers, and scientists alike.

Though it may be difficult to discern how specific ideas of *The Guide* have affected the wider academic community, Maimonides's rich interdisciplinary commitment offers a model to which most intellectuals aspire, but rarely achieve. In considering his own study of the great philosophers of his day, Maimonides quotes the wisdom of his Muslim contemporary Averroës to sum up his underlying conviction: "Listen to truth, no matter who pronounces it."[2] This motto is clearly present in *The Guide*, as Maimonides sought to impart his wisdom to his young student.

Maimonides's ideas were suited to his medieval context and offered a broad appeal to those seeking a balance between philosophical inquiry, reason, and faithfulness to religious tradition. Though many of his philosophical arguments based on Aristotle have been surpassed, *The Guide* is still a significant work of great intellect that was valued in its day.

Limitations

While *The Guide* does not have much significance in contemporary philosophical debate, the questions that it raises with regard to creation, the nature of divine omniscience and omnipotence, the appropriate language to use in speaking about God, and the chief end of humanity's goodness and happiness are still relevant today. For example, scholars involved in the contemporary debate concerning the origins of the universe (for instance, the theory of creation *ex nihilo**) continue to wrestle with the question of how scientific study relates to the biblical witness. Though Maimonides's work comes from a medieval context, it continues to challenge the notion that the two sides are irreconcilable.

Another universal issue that often comes up in modern contexts is the problem of evil and the nature of God's providence. In the light of droughts, earthquakes, and other natural disasters, people wrestle with the question: How could a good and all-powerful God allow such things to happen? Though one may not agree with Maimonides's conclusions, he addresses the subject in *The Guide* and tries to remain faithful to the Jewish belief that God is actively working on behalf of his people in space and time, even though this conflicts with Maimonides's philosophical position regarding God's foreknowledge and immutability.*

In terms of biblical and linguistic studies, Maimonides's exegesis continues to have value to students of the Bible today. His proficiency with language and his mastery of the Talmud and biblical texts forged a path that allowed for both literal and allegorical interpretation. Maimonides's logic and linguistic analysis laid the foundations for deconstructing the text and determining how terms predicated of God should be understood. Literal readings of the Bible—or other religious texts—continue today, but Maimonides's instructions on understanding the nature of linguistic utterances and how they reflect what we believe about God are still relevant in modern biblical studies.

NOTES

1   D. Yellin and I. Abrahams, *Maimonides* (Skokie, IL: Varda Books, 2002), 212.

2   I. Dobbs-Weinstein, et. al. *Maimonides and His Heritage* (New York: SUNY Press, 2009), p. x.

PLACE IN THE AUTHOR'S WORK

KEY POINTS

- Maimonides wrote widely on the subjects of philosophy, science, law, and medicine which influenced *The Guide of the Perplexed*.

- *The Guide* is considered Maimonides's most important work and the culmination of his wisdom and study.

- *The Guide* soon became a standard textbook for Jewish students of philosophy and influenced both Christian and Islamic scholars.

Positioning

Maimonides's *The Guide of the Perplexed* sits within an intellectual life and writings that were wide ranging. His earliest composition (1157-8) was a practical guide to the study of calendrical tables. By 1161, he had begun a larger work called *The Commentary on the Mishnah*. The Mishnah* is a compendium of Jewish law that was assembled around 200 c.e. It is divided into 63 tractates and became the basis for legal discussion in the rabbinic compilations of the Babylonian* and Jerusalem Talmud.* Maimonides's aim was to make an enormous body of Jewish legal literature accessible to people without formal training.

Around 1168, Maimonides composed one of his most significant works, the *Mishneh Torah* (or *Repetition of Torah*). This 14-volume code of Jewish law was written in eloquent Hebrew and provided a guide for average Jews regarding what the law required them to do and why they should do it. He reworked various passages from the Talmud and arranged the texts logically and simply so that they could be committed

> **❝** Maimonides was convinced that the people could be cajoled from a belief in the corporeal God to an incorporeal, more sophisticated belief, suggesting that even within a deterministic system, human beliefs can be modified. **❞**

Tamar Rudavsky, *Maimonides*

to memory. With this major work, Maimonides established himself as one of the great Jewish legal authorities of his time.

Maimonides studied extensively in philosophy, science, and Jewish law, and *The Guide* was the natural culmination of his scholarship. Written between 1185 and 1190, *The Guide* deals with the philosophical conception of God, arguments for the existence of God, and the problems associated with theodicy and providence, moral theory, and happiness. What is striking about *The Guide* compared to his earlier writings is that it is much less systematic in its form and often brings together unconnected subjects.[1] *The Guide* presents both the expertise of a Jewish rabbi and the highly trained mind of a philosopher, and many believe it is the climax of Maimonides's work.

Integration

Maimonides also wrote on other subjects in his letters and other compositions. His *Epistle to Yemen* was a pastoral letter to a persecuted Jewish community whom he encouraged to remain faithful despite their oppression. His *Letter on Astrology* was written to rabbis who were concerned with implications of astrological determinism* and its relationship to Jewish law. Maimonides also wrote extensively on the subject of resurrection.

In addition to being an expert on biblical, philosophical, and legal writings, he was also an accomplished physician and devoted much of his later life to medical treatises. Many of these works were translated into Hebrew and Latin and contributed to his fame abroad.[2]

In Jewish circles, the *Mishneh Torah* is still considered a great legal work, but *The Guide* has enjoyed a wider popularity overall. Considering his career as a physician in Egypt, Maimonides completed a diverse corpus of writings that influenced students of theology, philosophy, and science as well as those in the medical field.

Tracing Maimonides's intellectual life, it is not difficult to see how his love for Jewish law, biblical studies, philosophy, and the sciences all came through in his body of work. His life, study, and work reflect a love of learning that spanned a variety of disciplines but were ultimately bound together by his passion for understanding God and his creation.

Significance

Within a short time following Maimonides's death, *The Guide* had become a standard textbook for Jewish students of philosophy. His work, however, aggravated an existing tension between intellectually astute believers who wanted to understand the Bible in the light of philosophy and the natural sciences, and those of a simple faith who were more concerned with preserving traditional interpretation. *The Guide* was a watershed text that established the discipline of scientific and philosophical inquiry within the Jewish faith. *The Guide* also played a critical role in transitioning the works of Aristotle and Plato into the medieval Western world.

Another significant factor that contributed to the success of *The Guide* is that Maimonides did not present a dichotomy between the God of philosophy and the God of religion. Instead, he found philosophy integral to his Jewish faith and, while being unsatisfied with an abstract picture of God, clung firmly to the monotheism expressed in the biblical texts. Subsequent generations of critics may have surpassed the philosophical work of Maimonides, but his heritage continues thanks to his penetrating insights into Scripture and his conviction that the God of the Bible was also the God of the philosophers.

Other scholars have noted Maimonides's impact upon medieval scholastic thought and the important influence Maimonides had upon great thinkers such as Thomas Aquinas, Henry of Ghent* and others.[3] In his work on the impact of Maimonides upon thirteenth-century scholastic thought, Görge Hasselhoff* contends that Maimonides's influence stretched from philosophy to astronomy and to questions of biblical interpretation as well as medicine.[4] It is clear that *The Guide* paved the way for the philosophical study of religion soon after Maimonides's time, but its influence extended beyond Jewish thinkers and had an impact on Muslim and Christian scholars as well.

NOTES

1   Leo Strauss, "The Literary Character of the Guide for the Perplexed," in *Essays on Maimonides: An Octocentennial Volume*, ed. S.W. Baron (New York: Columbia University Press, 1941), 37–91.

2   Tamar Rudavsky, *Maimonides,* (Oxford: Wiley-Blackwell, 2010), 14-15.

3   Rudavsky, *Maimonides*, 12.

4   Görge K. Hasselhoff, "Maimonides in the Latin Middle Ages: An Introductory Survey," *Jewish Studies Quarterly,* 9 (2002): 1–20.

SECTION 3
IMPACT

MODULE 9
THE FIRST RESPONSES

KEY POINTS

*   Maimonides faced his greatest criticism from other rabbinic academies who viewed his work as an attack on traditional Judaism.

*   Maimonides offered some responses to his critics, but his declining health and seeming frustration with his opponents prevented him from fully entering into debate.

*   Though Maimonides addressed some of his critics, he did not alter his views and maintained his commitment to philosophy and religion.

Criticism

Like works by Aristotle and other Islamic philosophers, Maimonides's *The Guide of the Perplexed* depicted God's incorporeal nature as fundamental to any theological or philosophical discourse, which gave rise to substantial criticism. Given the importance he places on apophatic theology in *The Guide*, Maimonides was also criticized for his epistemological skepticism (in other words, his view that humans have a limited capacity for knowledge). Unsurprisingly, his most vocal opponents were rabbinic leaders who saw *The Guide* as an attack on Jewish belief. Rabbinic academies felt that Maimonides's naturalistic approach to prophecy and miracles threatened traditional Jewish belief in the exclusivity and intimacy of God's relationship with Israel.

In France and Spain, there were mixed reactions to *The Guide*. Some Jewish rabbis banned the study of Maimonides's works. This caused a wave of indignation from Maimonides's followers and

> 66 Like his Islamic forebears, Maimonides emphasized God's essential nature as uncaused, necessary, and absolutely simple. But his conclusions, which are so rooted in the incorporeality of the Deity, gave rise to substantial criticism among both Jewish and Christian thinkers. 99
>
> Tamar Rudavsky, *Maimonides*

resulted in two opposing camps in Jewish scholarship: those who rejected philosophical study and those who embraced it. The Ashkenazi Jews of northern France feared that the secular, philosophical teaching of *The Guide* undermined the essence of Judaism and that Maimonides had made God inaccessible and removed from religious experience. They argued for the possibility of intimacy between the worshipper and the divine through prayer and revelation, which led to a growing movement in Jewish mysticism.[1] In southern France, however, Maimonides's writings were readily adopted and taught.

Perhaps the most strident opposition to Maimonides came from the rabbinic academy in Baghdad. The principal of this academy wrote a 20-page treatise that criticized Maimonides on a number of points and accused him of denying the resurrection of the dead.[2] The treatise was given to Maimonides by his student Joseph ben Judah, who also entered into the controversy.

Responses

In response to the attacks from the Baghdad academy, Maimonides composed a letter in 1191 called *Treatise on the Resurrection*. In the letter, he provides a defense of his beliefs on immortality and the return of the soul to the body—many of which had already been written in *The Guide*.[3] He acknowledges that the public might have been confused about his position on the resurrection, but the tone of the letter is sarcastic, and it seems that Maimonides resented having to write again on a subject on which he had expounded in *The Guide*.[4]

He points out that his 13 articles of faith in *The Guide* sufficiently explain his position on life after death. The *Treatise on the Resurrection* was his only direct response to his attackers and gives us insight into a man who did not seem to have the strength to enter into extensive debate with his opponents.

Conflict And Consensus

A common theme among Maimonides's critics was that *The Guide* posed a threat to the traditional understanding of the Jewish religion. Since typical readings of Scripture relied on the interpretations of previous rabbis (as found in, for example, the Talmud) and God's particular revelation to the Jews, Maimonides's emphasis on secular thought stood in sharp contrast to the rabbinic academy. In many ways, Maimonides's critics highlight the perennial division between faith and reason, or simple belief versus scientific and philosophical inquiry.

Maimonides lived for 14 years after completing *The Guide*. During this period, his health was in decline and much of his time was devoted to his professional work as a physician in Cairo. He did expend some energy on more positive correspondence with Jews in southern France who embraced his works. In 1194, he wrote a letter in reply to questions he had received from scholars in Marseilles about his astrological views. He also wrote to Jonathan of Lunel,* whom he encouraged to remain steadfast in the study of the Talmud as well as in philosophical inquiry.[5]

Despite his critics, Maimonides did not revise his positions and continued to champion philosophy and the natural sciences as essential to understanding God, creation, and humanity, and to the pursuit of a happy life. Though future criticism would break down several of Maimonides's philosophical arguments, he succeeded in establishing philosophy as a legitimate pursuit for Jewish scholars of the biblical texts.

NOTES

1   Tamar Rudavsky, *Maimonides,* (Oxford: Wiley-Blackwell, 2010), 16.

2   Rudavsky, *Maimonides*, 12.

3   D. Yellin and I. Abrahams, *Maimonides,* (Skokie, IL: Varda Books, 2002), 194.

4   Rudavsky, *Maimonides*, 105-6.

5   Rudavsky, *Maimonides*, 12-15.

MODULE 10
THE EVOLVING DEBATE

KEY POINTS

- *The Guide of the Perplexed* has had continued influence from the medieval period until today both by scholars who accept and who reject Maimonides's ideas.

- No particular schools were formed after Maimonides, but his work has had significant influence in modern Jewish scholarship.

- Contemporary scholarship tends to focus on the style and function of the *Guide* and how Maimonides reveals, or conceals, esoteric truth.

Uses And Problems

Maimonides's *Guide of the Perplexed* had great influence in subsequent schools of Jewish thought as well as medieval Christian philosophy. Theologians were attracted to Maimonides's effort to locate the God of the Bible within the framework of Aristotelian and Platonic philosophy. Scholars such as Thomas Aquinas, Franciscan Alexander of Hales,* William of Auvergne,* and Albertus Magnus* were all influenced by *The Guide*.[1]

Much scholarship has also been devoted to Maimonides's influence in the life and work of the Dutch Jewish philosopher Baruch Spinoza* (1632–77). He carried out Maimonides's interpretative method to the fullest in his *Theologico-Political Treatise*. Spinoza's strategy, however, was exactly the opposite of Maimonides's approach. Whereas Maimonides tried to harmonize philosophical truth with Scripture, Spinoza found the task useless. Instead, Spinoza proposed an interpretative method of strict reliance on historical and linguistic analysis. Spinoza ultimately

> ❝ Maimonides emerges from the previous pages as a phenomenologist of religion who uses broad strokes of the brush to paint patterns of thought and behavior. He is a thinker who looks for absolute rules of the universe and humanity, an Aristotelian who tries to identify pure forms. ❞
>
> Sarah Stroumsa, *Maimonides in His World: Portrait of a Mediterranean Thinker*

rejected the Jewish faith and strove to liberate true philosophy from theology and religion. Thus, it is important to suggest that while signs of Maimonidean thought can be detected in Spinoza's philosophical works, he explicitly rejects the whole thrust of Maimonides's philosophical exegesis.[2]

The Guide continues in its influence today not because of its particular philosophical or religious arguments, important as those might be. Instead, *The Guide* offers a transition in the approach to religious tradition seen through the light of scientific advances and philosophical principles.

Schools Of Thought

The impact of *The Guide* extended throughout the medieval world particularly within Jewish rabbinic scholarship. Maimonides's method of interpretation was highly influential but did not develop into particular schools of thought. Moving into modern history, we see a pronounced influence of Maimonides on the great neo-Kantian* philosopher-mathematician Salomon Maimon* (1735–1800). Maimon, originally a Kabbalist,* or Jewish mystic, studied *The Guide* and at first criticized Maimonides's theory of the threefold unity of the intellect, but he later adopted it. Though Maimon was skeptical of Maimonides's belief in the perfection of humanity, he remained true to the Maimonidean argument of the subject-object unification through knowledge. In other words, he held that it was through the intellect that one might come into union with the divine. Though Maimon developed his own philosophical positions, he wrote that he viewed Maimonides as the "ideal of a perfect man."[3]

Another scholar, Moses Mendelssohn* (1729–86), who is often regarded as the first modern Jewish philosopher, began his philosophical studies with Maimonides and *The Guide*. The German-Jewish neo-Kantian philosopher Hermann Cohen* (1842–1918) was also influenced by Maimonides and stressed the moral, practical aspects of *The Guide*.[4] The list could go on, but it is enough to recall the significant influence *The Guide* has had over generations of philosophers and religious thinkers, especially within Judaism.

In Current Scholarship

Contemporary scholars have raised the question of how we should approach the esoteric truth set out in *The Guide* and to what extent its hidden knowledge can be understood. According to Leo Strauss,* an influential political philosopher who encouraged the contemporary application of medieval Islamic and Jewish philosophy, *The Guide* is deeply esoteric and must be interpreted as such.[5] Strauss's introduction to the Pines translation of *The Guide* stresses the fact that Maimonides wrote to sophisticated scholars and thus needed to conceal deeper truths from those reading *The Guide* on a popular level.[6] In the introduction to *The Guide*, Maimonides himself writes, "In speaking about very obscure matters it is necessary to conceal some parts and to disclose others."[7]

Other contemporary scholars, however, argue that *The Guide* should be read primarily as a dialectical work rather than an esoteric one. For example, Kenneth Seeskin* contends that *The Guide* does not contain one hidden truth, but offers "a patchwork of doctrines, conjectures and observations dealing with speculative matters."[8]

However readers approach *The Guide*, contemporary scholars and students of Maimonides will continue to wrestle with its contradictions and obscurities.

While scholars such as Strauss were committed to an academic study of *The Guide,* other Jewish intellectuals, such as Yeshayahu Leibowitz* (1903–94), focused on the religious implications of Maimonides's work in relation to Jewish legal practice and the end goal of knowing God. Leibowitz argued that Maimonides was, first and foremost, a Jew committed to observing the law and that he was only secondly a philosopher and scientist.[9] Thus *The Guide* for Leibowitz should be read as a religious book that emphasizes knowledge not for its own sake, but for the sake of drawing nearer to, and better understanding, God's glory.

NOTES

1   S. Feldman, "Maimonides- A Guide for Posterity," In *The Cambridge Companion to Maimonides*, ed. K. Seeskin (Cambridge: Cambridge University Press, 2005), 324.

2   Feldman, "Maimonides," 349-54.

3   Feldman, "Maimonides," 324, 354.

4   Feldman, "Maimonides," 355.

5   Tamar Rudavsky, *Maimonides,* (Oxford: Wiley-Blackwell, 2010), 23-24.

6   Maimonides, *The Guide of the Perplexed,* ed. Shlomo Pines (Chicago: University of Chicago Press, 1960), xi-xx.

7   Maimonides, *Guide*, Introduction, 10b.

8   Kenneth Seeskin, *Searching for a Distant God: The Legacy of Maimonides,*
(New York: Oxford University Press, 2000), 181.

9   P. Mendes-Flohr, "Maimonides in the Crucible of Zionism: Reflections on Yeshayahu Leibowitz's Negative Theology." In *Maimonides and His Heritage,* I. Dobbs-Weinstein, et. al. eds. (New York: SUNY Press, 2009), 181-92.

MODULE 11
IMPACT AND INFLUENCE TODAY

KEY POINTS

- *The Guide of the Perplexed* remains a seminal work today because of its foundational arguments in philosophy, science, and faith.

- Other medieval philosophers and theologians engaged with *The Guide* in both critical and positive ways.

- Maimonides raised significant questions about the nature of prophecy that continue to be debated today.

Position

Since Maimonides lived over 800 years ago, the impact of the *The Guide of the Perplexed* is limited in contemporary philosophical and religious studies. He still stands as a towering figure in Jewish faith, however, and *The Guide* remains the subject of much academic inquiry today.

Though *The Guide* is not part of the current intellectual debate in theological or philosophical studies, its universal themes still hold value for different faiths today. A critical theme in Maimonides's view was the use of anthropomorphic language in the Bible. He feared that passages in which God is depicted as having hands, ears, or a mouth could be misinterpreted by believers who would then be in danger of committing idolatry. Maimonides's philosophical pursuit of discovering the truth about God stood in contrast to the mystical approach, which relied mainly on the senses and experience. These two approaches to religious life—scholasticism* and mysticism*— have existed for centuries in Judaism, Christianity, and Islam, but Maimonides tried to find a middle road that combined rigorous

> **❝** I do not say that this Treatise will remove all difficulties for those who understand it. I do, however, say that it will remove most of the difficulties, and those of the greatest moment. **❞**
>
> Maimonides, *The Guide of the Perplexed*, Introduction

intellectual thought with spiritual and contemplative practice. Whether he was successful or not is still debated, yet he tried to maintain both reason and spirituality as he sought the truth.

Debates between religion and science continue in the contemporary world. Though *The Guide* is no longer used in these discussions, Maimonides provides a compelling argument that if we are to treat creation and metaphysics seriously, they must be undertaken in the light of theology and the truths that can be known about God. Maimonides demonstrated that the two fields of study are compatible and that, in fact, they lead to the same truth about God.

Interaction

The most significant challenges to *The Guide* came from the religious philosophers of subsequent centuries. The Jewish philosopher Gersonides argued that humans could speak meaningfully about God provided that the language used is understood equivocally rather than absolutely. Divine predicates represent the highest meaning of a term, and when the same term is applied to humans, it represents a lower meaning. Humans can demonstrate mercy, but God is perfect in mercy. Thus Gersonides contested Maimonides's apophatic methodology and believed that language used to describe God and humans shares a commonality, despite the fact that when used of God it refers to a primary, or perfect, reality.[1]

The Christian theologian and philosopher Thomas Aquinas (1225–74) agreed with Maimonides that it is impossible to know the essence of God's being, but he did believe that our language about God is meaningful. Indeed, Aquinas argued that we should not be limited to negative language when referring to the divine and contended that we can speak about God analogically. Like Gersonides, Aquinas did not believe that attributes of the divine (for example, God is good) could be predicated univocally of a transcendent God.[2] Yet terms like "good" were also not completely equivocal, and so Aquinas believed that theological language must be analogical—or somewhere between univocal and equivocal.

Another significant Jewish critic was Crescas (1340–1410), who did not dispute the existence or incorporeality of God but did not believe that these truths could be upheld by Aristotelian philosophy. Instead, Crescas argued that there cannot be an infinite chain of causes that terminates at a first cause, and that links in a causal chain need not be infinite.[3] This means that there does not have to be a prime mover and that the existence of God must be made through other arguments. His departure from Aristotle significantly undercut Maimonides's basic assumptions on the proofs of the existence and unity of God.

The Continuing Debate

Beyond particular philosophers and theologians, other Jewish groups were challenged by Maimonides's views in *The Guide.* One particular argument has to do with prophecy and the apparent universality that Maimonides presents. According to traditional Jewish belief, God chose Israel and its prophets to be his messengers. Maimonides, however, claimed that God's word was given to those who had achieved a level of intellectual perfection, which did not discriminate between Jew and non-Jew.[4] He also held that those who pursued intellectual perfection would draw near to the love of God, which, again, could be achieved by any person.

Maimonides did not discount Jewish law or the Scriptures, but he emphasized that obedience to God must be coupled with a contemplative life. Some denounced this as universalism, but it warrants consideration of the impact that living as a Jew in a Muslim nation had on Maimonides. He was a prominent rabbi and doctor in his community and had been trained under both Jews and Muslims. No doubt he served both Jews and Muslims in his medical capacity in Egypt and was able to enter into dialogue with Muslims throughout his life. His ability to hold firmly to his traditions while engaging those of different religious backgrounds might be seen as a positive example of how those from varying faiths can come together in dialogue and in serving one another.

NOTES

1   Tamar Rudavsky, *Maimonides,* (Oxford: Wiley-Blackwell, 2010), 56-57.

2   K. Seeskin. "Metaphysics and Its Transcendence." In *The Cambridge Companion to Maimonides,* edited by K. Seeskin, (Cambridge: Cambridge University Press, 2005), 82-100.

3   S. Feldman, "Maimonides- A Guide for Posterity." In *The Cambridge Companion to Maimonides*, ed. K. Seeskin, (Cambridge: Cambridge University Press, 2005), 340-45.

4   D. Yellin and I. Abrahams, *Maimonides,* (Skokie, IL: Varda Books, 2002), 181-2.

MODULE 12
WHERE NEXT?

KEY POINTS

- Maimonides was a Jewish scholar who embraced the intellectual developments of his world, whether Muslim or Christian.

- Maimonides's legacy will continue not only because of his philosophical expertise, but also because of his ability to synthesize wisdom from different cultures and religions.

- *The Guide of the Perplexed* will remain a seminal text because it addresses timeless topics of God, creation, and human happiness in a way that seeks to bridge science, philosophy, and faith.

Potential

Maimonides's *The Guide of the Perplexed* demonstrates his commitment to the universality of truth and allows his work to be accessed by all. By not requiring absolute belief in Jewish thought, Maimonides's *Guide* has the potential today to instruct Muslims, Christians, and even theists of various belief, provided that they are willing to adhere to his general philosophical method. *The Guide* also incorporates Maimonides's political philosophy, so others might learn from his legal thought as it engages with the biblical text. For the modern atheists or secularists who reject the existence of God, there might be less immediate application. Nevertheless, *The Guide* still remains relevant today despite the changes that have occurred in the 800 years since its writing.

Another point of potential stems from Maimonides's insight and openness to dialogue with thinkers from diverse religious, political, and ethnic backgrounds. As a student of Arabic philosophy, science,

> ❝For Maimonides, this [cultural] continuity seems to have been an undisputed fact. Some of the philosophical and religious traditions that shaped Maimonides' thought belonged to his contemporary world, where they all existed side by side and in continuous exchange and debate.❞
>
> Sarah Stroumsa, *Maimonides in His World*

and jurisprudence—as well as physician to the sultan*—Maimonides has become a positive symbol of assimilation in a culturally diverse world. He has come to represent the ideal polymath who remains faithful to his religious tradition. While this historical portrayal may not be completely accurate, Maimonides still holds a place in the minds of Jewish and secular thinkers as a model for holding faithfully to religious convictions while living in dialogue and community with others from different faiths.

In today's world, science and faith are frequently depicted as irreconcilable, and people often feel that they must choose one and abandon the other. Maimonides faced similar challenges—albeit in a very different cultural context—in medieval Andalusia and Egypt, which is one reason why he stands out as an exemplar of the possibility of religious faithfulness combined with intellectual growth and openness to new ideas.

Future Directions

Future academic study of *The Guide* will continue, but science and philosophy have moved on from medieval principles and understanding. When one considers the advancements that science has experienced in astronomy, biology, physics, and other sciences, can the philosophy of Maimonides still be useful in a contemporary context? It is true that if Maimonides were alive today witnessing atomic particles being smashed at high speeds, he would probably have to rethink his metaphysics. Yet despite rejecting his overarching metaphysical paradigm in *The Guide*, we can retain his rational method, which openly examined the world and Scripture. Such a spirit of inquiry led him to avoid authoritarianism, religious superstition, and intolerance.

It is likely that *The Guide* will continue to be considered a seminal text in the future. This is due not only to its content, but also to Maimonides's method and his extraordinary ability to creatively synthesize different disciplines into his teaching. What will also make *The Guide* a lasting text is its ambitious commitment to both the theoretical and the practical. Maimonides set out to create a work that would have an impact on a person's everyday life. *The Guide* is a text about how to pursue intellectual truths about God as they are revealed in creation and the Scriptures in order live the most abundant life possible.

Summary

The Guide remains a seminal text today because it opens a conversation between philosophy, science, and faith that seeks to reveal the mysteries of God and creation. Though his claims of truth might not be accepted in a post-modern world today, Maimonides encourages his students to pursue the deepest questions about God, the universe, and the meaning of life.

Whether in agreement with the principles laid out in *The Guide* or not, it is important to remember the context of Maimonides's life as a Jewish physician living and working in a Muslim country. Maimonides demonstrated that one can peacefully pursue intellectual freedom while remaining faithful to religious convictions and ethical living. For Maimonides, intellectual perfection was the noblest endeavor for all humankind. He was a man who combined theory and praxis. He remained a devout Jew and faithfully served his diverse community for years as a physician.

Like any great philosopher, Maimonides should not be judged on the philosophical questions that he solved but, rather, on the intellectual thought that he stimulated. *The Guide* is not a book of answers on God and the universe; it surveys the wisdom of science, philosophy, and Scripture to raise new questions and to encourage further exploration of the issues. Whether it is read in the twelfth or the twenty-first century, *The Guide* will continue to provoke questions about God and creation in such a way that its value will extend to future generations.

Maimonides's final words to his student Joseph at the end of *The Guide* sum up his desire for his pupil and for all who read his book:

> *God is very near to everyone who calls,*
> *If he calls truly and has no distractions;*
> *He is found by every seeker who searches for Him,*
> *If he marches toward Him and goes not astray.*[1]

NOTES

1   Maimonides, *The Guide of the Perplexed,* ed. Shlomo Pines, (Chicago: University of Chicago Press, 1960), III:54.

GLOSSARY

GLOSSARY OF TERMS

Almohads: Berber in origin, the Almohads were puritanical Muslims* who rose up against the corrupt Almoravids in southern Morocco in the twelfth century and ruled Spain and all Maghrib from around 1147 until about 1213.

Anthropomorphic (also **anthropomorphism**, n.): ascribing human form or characteristics to non-human things.

Apophatic theology: a view that holds that one can only speak of God by discussing his negative attributes rather than his positive attributes (e.g., God is not evil, God is not physical, God is not bound by time, etc.).

Aristotelian: having to do with the philosophy of Aristotle.*

Ashkenazi: a community of diaspora Jews* who settled in Europe and developed their own traditions and particular way of life.

Babylon (also **Babylonian,** adj.): An ancient Mesopotamian city in modern-day Iraq. Many Jews* lived there in exile after Jerusalem was destroyed by the Babylonians in 587 BCE.

Bible: the sacred texts of the Jewish* and Christian* religions. The Old Testament, or Hebrew Bible, consists of sixty-six books and is used by Jews. The New Testament consists of twenty-seven books. Both Old and New Testaments are used by Christians.

Caliph: the chief Muslim* religious ruler who is often regarded as the successor to Muhammad, the founder of Islam.*

Christian: a person who believes and follows the teachings of Christianity.

Corporeal: relating to a person's body as opposed to the spirit.

Cosmogony: the area of science that deals with the origins of the universe.

Cosmology: the area of science that deals with astronomy and particle physics in the study of the universe and solar system.

Determinism: the philosophical doctrine that regards all events to be determined. Human action is, therefore, not free but determined by motives and causes external to the human will.

Epistemology: the study of knowledge and how we are able to know things and justify our beliefs.

Exegesis: the exposition or analysis of the Bible* to determine its meaning.

Ex nihilo: out of, or from, nothing.

Gentile: a person not belonging to one's religious community and often used to refer to those who are non-Jews.

Immutability: the quality of being unchanging or unable to be changed over time.

Incorporeal (also **incorporeality**, n.): relating to that which is non-bodily or material such as the spirit.

Islam (also **Islamic**, adj.): the Muslim* religion based on the teachings of the prophet Muhammad who worshipped one God, Allah.

Ismā'īlī: an Islamic* sect that emphasized apophatic theology* and believed that at the heart of all religions there was a single philosophic truth, which promoted an ethos of free inquiry and the study of philosophy and the sciences.

Judaism (also **Jewish**, adj.): the religion of the Jewish people who follow the teachings of Moses.* This monotheistic religion dates back to the patriarch Abraham with detailed histories contained in the Old Testament.

Kabbalist: a Jew* who practices the tradition of mystical interpretation of the Bible.*

Kalām: an Islamic* philosophical practice that deals with the interpretation of religious doctrines through debate and discourse. During Maimonides's lifetime, there were several different schools of *kalām* thought.

Mishnah: is the authoritative collection of rabbinical* writings on the interpretation of the Jewish* law found in the Old Testament.

Muslim: those who follow the teachings of Islam.*

Mutakallimūn: followers of the Islamic* principles of *kalām** who discussed philosophy, theology, and interpretation of the Quran.

Mysticism: the belief that one can be unified with god through the spirit and not through knowledge or intellect.

Neo-Kantian: a philosophical position based on the philosophy of Immanuel Kant (1724-1804), a German philosopher who was known for his most significant work, *Critique of Pure Reason*. Kant argued that human experience was formed by our minds and was integral to our concepts of space/time and cause/effect.

Neoplatonic: Neoplatonism combined ideas from Plato,* Aristotle,* Pythagoras, and the Stoics with oriental mysticism. It was a major influence on early Christian* writers and posited that the soul could rise above the material world through virtue and contemplation.

Rabbi (also **rabbinic, rabbinical**, adj.): a Jewish* scholar or religious leader who is an expert in Jewish law.

Scholasticism: theology and philosophy taught in medieval Europe that was based on the teachings of Aristotle* and placed a strong emphasis on dogma and tradition.

Scripture: another way of referring to the Bible* or sacred texts from different religious beliefs.

Shema: a Hebrew prayer from the Torah* recited daily by Jews* and one of the core confessions of Judaism.*

Sultan: the term used for a Muslim* king or sovereign.

Talmud: the Babylonian and Jerusalem Talmud are two similar collections of Jewish* civil and religious law that include the Mishnah* and Gemara.* The rabbinic* teachings are central to the Jewish faith.

Theodicy: the defense of divine goodness and providence despite the existence of evil.

Trinity: the Christian* belief that God consists of three persons in perfect unity: the Father, the Son, and the Holy Spirit.

Torah: a Jewish* term used to describe the first five books of the Bible.*

PEOPLE MENTIONED IN THE TEXT

'Abd ar-Rahman III (889-961) was the Caliph of Córdoba from 912–961 in Andalusia, Spain. He was one of the great rulers of the Umayyad dynasty and was known for his religious tolerance.

Abū Bakr Ibn Bājja (also called Avempace) (c. 1085-1138) was a medieval writer in Andalusia who wrote on philosophical topics and also produced works on astronomy, physics, music, medicine, and botany. He was also known as a great poet.

Al-Fārābī (c. 872–951) was an Islamic* philosopher and scientist who composed works in the area of political philosophy and metaphysics. Some of his notable works are *The Great Book of Music* and *On the Introduction of Knowledge*.

Al-Ghazali (c. 1058–1111) was a Muslim* theologian and philosopher of Persian decent who defended Islam* against forms of Neoplatonism.* He is considered one of the most influential Muslims after Muhammad.

Al-Qādī al-Fādil al-Baysani (1135–1200) was Maimonides's patron. He was a poet, administrator, statesman, and scholar who had amassed a collection of Arabic works.

Alexander of Aphrodisias (c. 200) was a Greek philosopher and commentator on the works of Aristotle.* He taught in Athens and became head of the Peripatetic school.

Al-Qifti (c. 1172-1248) was a Muslim* historian from Egypt who is most remembered for his bibliographic work of physicians, astronomers, and philosophers called *The History of Learned Men*.

Thomas Aquinas (1225–1274) was a Dominican friar and a Doctor of the Church. He was one of the most influential medieval theologians of the Catholic Church and his most celebrated work is the *Summa Theologiae*. He is considered one of Christianity's* greatest theologians and philosophers.

Aristotle (384-322 B.C.E.) was an ancient Greek philosopher who was tutor to Alexander the Great. Aristotle's philosophy and metaphysics had a profound influence on the Western world.

William of Auvergne (1190-1249) was a French priest who was the bishop of Paris from 1228 till his death. He was a highly regarded scholar and philosopher who wrote widely on theological subjects.

Averroës (1126-1198) was an Islamic* polymath who lived in southern Spain. He wrote broadly on Aristotle,* Islamic law and theology, mathematics, astronomy, physics, and music.

Avicenna (c. 980-1037) was a Persian Islamic* philosopher who also excelled in physics, astronomy, and medicine. He is most renowned for his works *The Book of Healing* and *The Canon of Medicine* which became standard texts in medical universities.

Hermann Cohen (1842–1918) was a German–Jewish* philosopher who founded the neo-Kantian* Marburg school. Considered one of the great nineteenth-century philosophers, he produced three volumes of his systematic work: *Logik der reinen Erkenntnis*, *Ethik des reinen Willens*, and *Ästhetik des reinen Gefühls*.

Crescas (1340–1410) was a Spanish-Jewish* philosopher who promoted a rationalistic approach to the study of Jewish law. His classic work *The Light of the Lord* was a refutation of Aristotelian* philosophical principles.

Ezekiel (c. 587 BCE) was a Jewish* prophet and priest who was a part of the exile to Babylon.* His prophecies are recorded in the Old Testament.

Gersonides (1288–1344) was a medieval French-Jewish* philosopher, mathematician, and astronomer. His most celebrated work, *The Wars of the Lord*, was modeled after Maimonides's *Guide* as it adhered to Aristotelian* thought.

Henry of Ghent (c. 1217-1293) was a medieval scholastic philosopher and theologian who was known for his writings on the being of essence in humanity which came first from God before humans come into actual, physical existence.

Alexander of Hales (c. 1185-1245) was a philosopher and theologian who played a significant role in the scholastic movement during the medieval period. He joined the Franciscan monastic order and was known for his writings on the doctrine of the sacraments.

Görge K. Hasselhoff is a contemporary scholar.

Ibn Tumart (c. 1080-1128) was a Muslim* scholar from Morocco and a political leader who established the strict religious movement of the Almohads.* He led a revolt against the ruling Almoravids around 1120.

Joseph ben Judah (c. 1160-1226) was a Jewish* physician and poet and was a disciple of Maimonides.

Jonathan of Lunel (c. 1135-1210) was a French-Jewish* philosopher who defended the works of Maimonides and also produced his own commentary on the work of Alfasi, a Jewish rabbi and scholar, as well as other rabbinic★ works.

Yeshayahu Leibowitz (1903–1994) was an Israeli Jewish* professor of organic chemistry at Hebrew University in Jerusalem. As an orthodox Jew, he was also known for his outspoken religious and political views. He authored a wide range of books on philosophy, politics, and on Maimonides.

Albertus Magnus (c. 1200-80) was a theologian in the Dominican monastic order and was a noted philosopher, scientist, and theologian. He pioneered the Christian* study of Aristotle* and later was the teacher of Thomas Aquinas.*

Salomon Maimon (1735–1800) was a German-Jewish* philosopher who explored Kabbalah,* or Jewish mysticism. He settled in Berlin and was known as one of Immanuel Kant's most significant critics.

Moses Mendelssohn (1729–1786) is often regarded as the first modern Jewish* philosopher. He was educated in German thought and wrote on philosophy and metaphysics. One of his celebrated works was *On the Immortality of Souls*, which was modeled on Plato's *Phaedo*.

Moses (c. 1400 B.C.E.) is the primary leader of the Israelites who led them from captivity in Egypt to the edge of the Promised Land in southern Palestine. His works are recorded in the first five books of the Bible called the Pentateuch.

Plato (c. 428-348 B.C.E.) was a classic Greek philosopher who founded the academy in Athens. He is considered the most significant philosopher in the Western world whose works such as *The Republic* are still widely studied today.

Kenneth Seeskin (b. 1947) is the Philip M. and Ethel Klutznick Professor of Jewish Civilization at Northwestern University. He is the author and editor of several books on Maimonides, including *The Cambridge Companion to Maimonides*.

Baruch Spinoza (1632–77) was a Dutch-Jewish* philosopher and father of modern biblical criticism. His most famous work, *Ethics*, refuted some of Descartes' philosophy and offered a pantheistic view of God.

Leo Strauss (1899–1973) was an influential political philosopher who encouraged the contemporary application of medieval Islamic* and Jewish* philosophy. He was professor of science at the University of Chicago.

Themistius (c. 390) was a Greek philosopher and rhetorician. He was a politician who served in Constantinople and was known for his commentaries on the works of Aristotle.*

Samuel ibn Tibbon (c. 1150–c. 1230) was also known as Samuel ben Judah and lived in the Provence region of southern France. He was a Jewish* philosopher and skilled linguist who translated Maimonides's works.

WORKS CITED

WORKS CITED

Davidson, Herbert A., *Moses Maimonides: The Man and his Works*. Oxford: Oxford University Press, 2005.

Dobbs-Weinstein, I., L. E. Goodman and J. A. Grady, eds. *Maimonides and His Heritage*. New York: SUNY Press, 2009.

Feldman, Seymour. "Maimonides: A Guide for Posterity." In *The Cambridge Companion to Maimonides*, edited by K. Seeskin, 324-59. Cambridge: Cambridge University Press, 2005.

Hasselhoff, Görge K. "Maimonides in the Latin Middle Ages: An Introductory Survey." *Jewish Studies Quarterly* 9 (2002): 1–20.

Green, Kenneth H. *Leo Strauss and the Rediscovery of Maimonides.* Chicago: University of Chicago Press, 2013.

Kraemer, Joel L. "Moses Maimonides: An Intellectual Portrait." In *The Cambridge Companion to Maimonides*, edited by K. Seeskin, 10–57. Cambridge: Cambridge University Press, 2005.

Kraemer, Joel L. *Maimonides: The Life and World of One of Civilization's Greatest Minds.* New York: Doubleday Press, 2008.

Maimonides. *The Guide of the Perplexed*. edited by Shlomo Pines. Chicago: University of Chicago Press, 1963.

Manekin, Charles H. "Divine Will in Maimonides's Later Writings." In *Maimonidean Studies*, edited by A. Hyman and A. Ivry, 189–222. New Jersey: Ktav, 2008.

Marx, Alexander. "Texts by and About Maimonides." *Jewish Quarterly Review N.S.* 25 (1934): 374–81.

Mendes-Flohr, Paul. "Maimonides in the Crucible of Zionism: Reflections on Yeshayahu Leibowitz's Negative Theology." In *Maimonides and His Heritage,* edited by I. Dobbs-Weinstein, et. al. 181-92. New York, SUNY Press, 2009.

Pines, Shlomo. "The Limitations of Knowledge According to Al-Farabi, Ibn Bajja, and Maimonides." In *Studies in Medieval Jewish History and Literature*, edited by I. Twersky, 82–109. Cambridge, MA: Harvard University Press, 1979.

Rudavsky, Tamar M. *Maimonides*. Oxford: Wiley-Blackwell, 2010.

Seeskin, Kenneth. *Searching for a Distant God: The Legacy of Maimonides*. New York: Oxford University Press, 2000.

Seeskin, Kenneth, ed. *The Cambridge Companion to Maimonides.* Cambridge: Cambridge University Press, 2005.

Seeskin, Kenneth. "Metaphysics and Its Transcendence." In *The Cambridge Companion to Maimonides,* 82-104, edited by K. Seeskin. Cambridge: Cambridge University Press, 2005.

Shatz, David. "Maimonides's Moral Theory." In *The Cambridge Companion to Maimonides*, edited by K. Seeskin, 167–93. Cambridge: Cambridge University Press, 2005.

Strauss, Leo. "The Literary Character of the Guide for the Perplexed." In *Essays on Maimonides: An Octocentennial Volume*, edited by S. W. Baron, 37–91. New York: Columbia University Press, 1941.

Stroumsa, Sarah, *Maimonides in His World: Portrait of a Mediterranean Thinker*. Princeton, NJ: Princeton University Press, 2009.

Tepper, Aryeh. *Progressive Minds, Conservative Politics: Leo Strauss's Later Writings on Maimonides*. Albany: State University of New York Press, 2013.

Yellin, D., and I. Abrahams. *Maimonides*. Skokie, IL: Varda Books, 2002.

THE MACAT LIBRARY
BY DISCIPLINE

AFRICANA STUDIES

Chinua Achebe's *An Image of Africa: Racism in Conrad's Heart of Darkness*
W. E. B. Du Bois's *The Souls of Black Folk*
Zora Neale Huston's *Characteristics of Negro Expression*
Martin Luther King Jr's *Why We Can't Wait*
Toni Morrison's *Playing in the Dark: Whiteness in the American Literary Imagination*

ANTHROPOLOGY

Arjun Appadurai's *Modernity at Large: Cultural Dimensions of Globalisation*
Philippe Ariès's *Centuries of Childhood*
Franz Boas's *Race, Language and Culture*
Kim Chan & Renée Mauborgne's *Blue Ocean Strategy*
Jared Diamond's *Guns, Germs & Steel: the Fate of Human Societies*
Jared Diamond's *Collapse: How Societies Choose to Fail or Survive*
E. E. Evans-Pritchard's *Witchcraft, Oracles and Magic Among the Azande*
James Ferguson's *The Anti-Politics Machine*
Clifford Geertz's *The Interpretation of Cultures*
David Graeber's *Debt: the First 5000 Years*
Karen Ho's *Liquidated: An Ethnography of Wall Street*
Geert Hofstede's *Culture's Consequences: Comparing Values, Behaviors, Institutes and Organizations across Nations*
Claude Lévi-Strauss's *Structural Anthropology*
Jay Macleod's *Ain't No Makin' It: Aspirations and Attainment in a Low-Income Neighborhood*
Saba Mahmood's *The Politics of Piety: The Islamic Revival and the Feminist Subject*
Marcel Mauss's *The Gift*

BUSINESS

Jean Lave & Etienne Wenger's *Situated Learning*
Theodore Levitt's *Marketing Myopia*
Burton G. Malkiel's *A Random Walk Down Wall Street*
Douglas McGregor's *The Human Side of Enterprise*
Michael Porter's *Competitive Strategy: Creating and Sustaining Superior Performance*
John Kotter's *Leading Change*
C. K. Prahalad & Gary Hamel's *The Core Competence of the Corporation*

CRIMINOLOGY

Michelle Alexander's *The New Jim Crow: Mass Incarceration in the Age of Colorblindness*
Michael R. Gottfredson & Travis Hirschi's *A General Theory of Crime*
Richard Herrnstein & Charles A. Murray's *The Bell Curve: Intelligence and Class Structure in American Life*
Elizabeth Loftus's *Eyewitness Testimony*
Jay Macleod's *Ain't No Makin' It: Aspirations and Attainment in a Low-Income Neighborhood*
Philip Zimbardo's *The Lucifer Effect*

ECONOMICS

Janet Abu-Lughod's *Before European Hegemony*
Ha-Joon Chang's *Kicking Away the Ladder*
David Brion Davis's *The Problem of Slavery in the Age of Revolution*
Milton Friedman's *The Role of Monetary Policy*
Milton Friedman's *Capitalism and Freedom*
David Graeber's *Debt: the First 5000 Years*
Friedrich Hayek's *The Road to Serfdom*
Karen Ho's *Liquidated: An Ethnography of Wall Street*

John Maynard Keynes's *The General Theory of Employment, Interest and Money*
Charles P. Kindleberger's *Manias, Panics and Crashes*
Robert Lucas's *Why Doesn't Capital Flow from Rich to Poor Countries?*
Burton G. Malkiel's *A Random Walk Down Wall Street*
Thomas Robert Malthus's *An Essay on the Principle of Population*
Karl Marx's *Capital*
Thomas Piketty's *Capital in the Twenty-First Century*
Amartya Sen's *Development as Freedom*
Adam Smith's *The Wealth of Nations*
Nassim Nicholas Taleb's *The Black Swan: The Impact of the Highly Improbable*
Amos Tversky's & Daniel Kahneman's *Judgment under Uncertainty: Heuristics and Biases*
Mahbub Ul Haq's *Reflections on Human Development*
Max Weber's *The Protestant Ethic and the Spirit of Capitalism*

FEMINISM AND GENDER STUDIES

Judith Butler's *Gender Trouble*
Simone De Beauvoir's *The Second Sex*
Michel Foucault's *History of Sexuality*
Betty Friedan's *The Feminine Mystique*
Saba Mahmood's *The Politics of Piety: The Islamic Revival and the Feminist Subject*
Joan Wallach Scott's *Gender and the Politics of History*
Mary Wollstonecraft's *A Vindication of the Rights of Woman*
Virginia Woolf's *A Room of One's Own*

GEOGRAPHY

The Brundtland Report's *Our Common Future*
Rachel Carson's *Silent Spring*
Charles Darwin's *On the Origin of Species*
James Ferguson's *The Anti-Politics Machine*
Jane Jacobs's *The Death and Life of Great American Cities*
James Lovelock's *Gaia: A New Look at Life on Earth*
Amartya Sen's *Development as Freedom*
Mathis Wackernagel & William Rees's *Our Ecological Footprint*

HISTORY

Janet Abu-Lughod's *Before European Hegemony*
Benedict Anderson's *Imagined Communities*
Bernard Bailyn's *The Ideological Origins of the American Revolution*
Hanna Batatu's *The Old Social Classes And The Revolutionary Movements Of Iraq*
Christopher Browning's *Ordinary Men: Reserve Police Batallion 101 and the Final Solution in Poland*
Edmund Burke's *Reflections on the Revolution in France*
William Cronon's *Nature's Metropolis: Chicago And The Great West*
Alfred W. Crosby's *The Columbian Exchange*
Hamid Dabashi's *Iran: A People Interrupted*
David Brion Davis's *The Problem of Slavery in the Age of Revolution*
Nathalie Zemon Davis's *The Return of Martin Guerre*
Jared Diamond's *Guns, Germs & Steel: the Fate of Human Societies*
Frank Dikotter's *Mao's Great Famine*
John W Dower's *War Without Mercy: Race And Power In The Pacific War*
W. E. B. Du Bois's *The Souls of Black Folk*
Richard J. Evans's *In Defence of History*
Lucien Febvre's *The Problem of Unbelief in the 16th Century*
Sheila Fitzpatrick's *Everyday Stalinism*

The Macat Library By Discipline

Eric Foner's *Reconstruction: America's Unfinished Revolution, 1863-1877*
Michel Foucault's *Discipline and Punish*
Michel Foucault's *History of Sexuality*
Francis Fukuyama's *The End of History and the Last Man*
John Lewis Gaddis's *We Now Know: Rethinking Cold War History*
Ernest Gellner's *Nations and Nationalism*
Eugene Genovese's *Roll, Jordan, Roll: The World the Slaves Made*
Carlo Ginzburg's *The Night Battles*
Daniel Goldhagen's *Hitler's Willing Executioners*
Jack Goldstone's *Revolution and Rebellion in the Early Modern World*
Antonio Gramsci's *The Prison Notebooks*
Alexander Hamilton, John Jay & James Madison's *The Federalist Papers*
Christopher Hill's *The World Turned Upside Down*
Carole Hillenbrand's *The Crusades: Islamic Perspectives*
Thomas Hobbes's *Leviathan*
Eric Hobsbawm's *The Age Of Revolution*
John A. Hobson's *Imperialism: A Study*
Albert Hourani's *History of the Arab Peoples*
Samuel P. Huntington's *The Clash of Civilizations and the Remaking of World Order*
C. L. R. James's *The Black Jacobins*
Tony Judt's *Postwar: A History of Europe Since 1945*
Ernst Kantorowicz's *The King's Two Bodies: A Study in Medieval Political Theology*
Paul Kennedy's *The Rise and Fall of the Great Powers*
Ian Kershaw's *The "Hitler Myth": Image and Reality in the Third Reich*
John Maynard Keynes's *The General Theory of Employment, Interest and Money*
Charles P. Kindleberger's *Manias, Panics and Crashes*
Martin Luther King Jr's *Why We Can't Wait*
Henry Kissinger's *World Order: Reflections on the Character of Nations and the Course of History*
Thomas Kuhn's *The Structure of Scientific Revolutions*
Georges Lefebvre's *The Coming of the French Revolution*
John Locke's *Two Treatises of Government*
Niccolò Machiavelli's *The Prince*
Thomas Robert Malthus's *An Essay on the Principle of Population*
Mahmood Mamdani's *Citizen and Subject: Contemporary Africa And The Legacy Of Late Colonialism*
Karl Marx's *Capital*
Stanley Milgram's *Obedience to Authority*
John Stuart Mill's *On Liberty*
Thomas Paine's *Common Sense*
Thomas Paine's *Rights of Man*
Geoffrey Parker's *Global Crisis: War, Climate Change and Catastrophe in the Seventeenth Century*
Jonathan Riley-Smith's *The First Crusade and the Idea of Crusading*
Jean-Jacques Rousseau's *The Social Contract*
Joan Wallach Scott's *Gender and the Politics of History*
Theda Skocpol's *States and Social Revolutions*
Adam Smith's *The Wealth of Nations*
Timothy Snyder's *Bloodlands: Europe Between Hitler and Stalin*
Sun Tzu's *The Art of War*
Keith Thomas's *Religion and the Decline of Magic*
Thucydides's *The History of the Peloponnesian War*
Frederick Jackson Turner's *The Significance of the Frontier in American History*
Odd Arne Westad's *The Global Cold War: Third World Interventions And The Making Of Our Times*

LITERATURE

Chinua Achebe's *An Image of Africa: Racism in Conrad's Heart of Darkness*
Roland Barthes's *Mythologies*
Homi K. Bhabha's *The Location of Culture*
Judith Butler's *Gender Trouble*
Simone De Beauvoir's *The Second Sex*
Ferdinand De Saussure's *Course in General Linguistics*
T. S. Eliot's *The Sacred Wood: Essays on Poetry and Criticism*
Zora Neale Huston's *Characteristics of Negro Expression*
Toni Morrison's *Playing in the Dark: Whiteness in the American Literary Imagination*
Edward Said's *Orientalism*
Gayatri Chakravorty Spivak's *Can the Subaltern Speak?*
Mary Wollstonecraft's *A Vindication of the Rights of Women*
Virginia Woolf's *A Room of One's Own*

PHILOSOPHY

Elizabeth Anscombe's *Modern Moral Philosophy*
Hannah Arendt's *The Human Condition*
Aristotle's *Metaphysics*
Aristotle's *Nicomachean Ethics*
Edmund Gettier's *Is Justified True Belief Knowledge?*
Georg Wilhelm Friedrich Hegel's *Phenomenology of Spirit*
David Hume's *Dialogues Concerning Natural Religion*
David Hume's *The Enquiry for Human Understanding*
Immanuel Kant's *Religion within the Boundaries of Mere Reason*
Immanuel Kant's *Critique of Pure Reason*
Søren Kierkegaard's *The Sickness Unto Death*
Søren Kierkegaard's *Fear and Trembling*
C. S. Lewis's *The Abolition of Man*
Alasdair MacIntyre's *After Virtue*
Marcus Aurelius's *Meditations*
Friedrich Nietzsche's *On the Genealogy of Morality*
Friedrich Nietzsche's *Beyond Good and Evil*
Plato's *Republic*
Plato's *Symposium*
Jean-Jacques Rousseau's *The Social Contract*
Gilbert Ryle's *The Concept of Mind*
Baruch Spinoza's *Ethics*
Sun Tzu's *The Art of War*
Ludwig Wittgenstein's *Philosophical Investigations*

POLITICS

Benedict Anderson's *Imagined Communities*
Aristotle's *Politics*
Bernard Bailyn's *The Ideological Origins of the American Revolution*
Edmund Burke's *Reflections on the Revolution in France*
John C. Calhoun's *A Disquisition on Government*
Ha-Joon Chang's *Kicking Away the Ladder*
Hamid Dabashi's *Iran: A People Interrupted*
Hamid Dabashi's *Theology of Discontent: The Ideological Foundation of the Islamic Revolution in Iran*
Robert Dahl's *Democracy and its Critics*
Robert Dahl's *Who Governs?*
David Brion Davis's *The Problem of Slavery in the Age of Revolution*

The Macat Library By Discipline

Alexis De Tocqueville's *Democracy in America*
James Ferguson's *The Anti-Politics Machine*
Frank Dikotter's *Mao's Great Famine*
Sheila Fitzpatrick's *Everyday Stalinism*
Eric Foner's *Reconstruction: America's Unfinished Revolution, 1863-1877*
Milton Friedman's *Capitalism and Freedom*
Francis Fukuyama's *The End of History and the Last Man*
John Lewis Gaddis's *We Now Know: Rethinking Cold War History*
Ernest Gellner's *Nations and Nationalism*
David Graeber's *Debt: the First 5000 Years*
Antonio Gramsci's *The Prison Notebooks*
Alexander Hamilton, John Jay & James Madison's *The Federalist Papers*
Friedrich Hayek's *The Road to Serfdom*
Christopher Hill's *The World Turned Upside Down*
Thomas Hobbes's *Leviathan*
John A. Hobson's *Imperialism: A Study*
Samuel P. Huntington's *The Clash of Civilizations and the Remaking of World Order*
Tony Judt's *Postwar: A History of Europe Since 1945*
David C. Kang's *China Rising: Peace, Power and Order in East Asia*
Paul Kennedy's *The Rise and Fall of Great Powers*
Robert Keohane's *After Hegemony*
Martin Luther King Jr.'s *Why We Can't Wait*
Henry Kissinger's *World Order: Reflections on the Character of Nations and the Course of History*
John Locke's *Two Treatises of Government*
Niccolò Machiavelli's *The Prince*
Thomas Robert Malthus's *An Essay on the Principle of Population*
Mahmood Mamdani's *Citizen and Subject: Contemporary Africa And The Legacy Of Late Colonialism*
Karl Marx's *Capital*
John Stuart Mill's *On Liberty*
John Stuart Mill's *Utilitarianism*
Hans Morgenthau's *Politics Among Nations*
Thomas Paine's *Common Sense*
Thomas Paine's *Rights of Man*
Thomas Piketty's *Capital in the Twenty-First Century*
Robert D. Putman's *Bowling Alone*
John Rawls's *Theory of Justice*
Jean-Jacques Rousseau's *The Social Contract*
Theda Skocpol's *States and Social Revolutions*
Adam Smith's *The Wealth of Nations*
Sun Tzu's *The Art of War*
Henry David Thoreau's *Civil Disobedience*
Thucydides's *The History of the Peloponnesian War*
Kenneth Waltz's *Theory of International Politics*
Max Weber's *Politics as a Vocation*
Odd Arne Westad's *The Global Cold War: Third World Interventions And The Making Of Our Times*

POSTCOLONIAL STUDIES

Roland Barthes's *Mythologies*
Frantz Fanon's *Black Skin, White Masks*
Homi K. Bhabha's *The Location of Culture*
Gustavo Gutiérrez's *A Theology of Liberation*
Edward Said's *Orientalism*
Gayatri Chakravorty Spivak's *Can the Subaltern Speak?*

PSYCHOLOGY

Gordon Allport's *The Nature of Prejudice*
Alan Baddeley & Graham Hitch's *Aggression: A Social Learning Analysis*
Albert Bandura's *Aggression: A Social Learning Analysis*
Leon Festinger's *A Theory of Cognitive Dissonance*
Sigmund Freud's *The Interpretation of Dreams*
Betty Friedan's *The Feminine Mystique*
Michael R. Gottfredson & Travis Hirschi's *A General Theory of Crime*
Eric Hoffer's *The True Believer: Thoughts on the Nature of Mass Movements*
William James's *Principles of Psychology*
Elizabeth Loftus's *Eyewitness Testimony*
A. H. Maslow's *A Theory of Human Motivation*
Stanley Milgram's *Obedience to Authority*
Steven Pinker's *The Better Angels of Our Nature*
Oliver Sacks's *The Man Who Mistook His Wife For a Hat*
Richard Thaler & Cass Sunstein's *Nudge: Improving Decisions About Health, Wealth and Happiness*
Amos Tversky's *Judgment under Uncertainty: Heuristics and Biases*
Philip Zimbardo's *The Lucifer Effect*

SCIENCE

Rachel Carson's *Silent Spring*
William Cronon's *Nature's Metropolis: Chicago And The Great West*
Alfred W. Crosby's *The Columbian Exchange*
Charles Darwin's *On the Origin of Species*
Richard Dawkin's *The Selfish Gene*
Thomas Kuhn's *The Structure of Scientific Revolutions*
Geoffrey Parker's *Global Crisis: War, Climate Change and Catastrophe in the Seventeenth Century*
Mathis Wackernagel & William Rees's *Our Ecological Footprint*

SOCIOLOGY

Michelle Alexander's *The New Jim Crow: Mass Incarceration in the Age of Colorblindness*
Gordon Allport's *The Nature of Prejudice*
Albert Bandura's *Aggression: A Social Learning Analysis*
Hanna Batatu's *The Old Social Classes And The Revolutionary Movements Of Iraq*
Ha-Joon Chang's *Kicking Away the Ladder*
W. E. B. Du Bois's *The Souls of Black Folk*
Émile Durkheim's *On Suicide*
Frantz Fanon's *Black Skin, White Masks*
Frantz Fanon's *The Wretched of the Earth*
Eric Foner's *Reconstruction: America's Unfinished Revolution, 1863-1877*
Eugene Genovese's *Roll, Jordan, Roll: The World the Slaves Made*
Jack Goldstone's *Revolution and Rebellion in the Early Modern World*
Antonio Gramsci's *The Prison Notebooks*
Richard Herrnstein & Charles A Murray's *The Bell Curve: Intelligence and Class Structure in American Life*
Eric Hoffer's *The True Believer: Thoughts on the Nature of Mass Movements*
Jane Jacobs's *The Death and Life of Great American Cities*
Robert Lucas's *Why Doesn't Capital Flow from Rich to Poor Countries?*
Jay Macleod's *Ain't No Makin' It: Aspirations and Attainment in a Low Income Neighborhood*
Elaine May's *Homeward Bound: American Families in the Cold War Era*
Douglas McGregor's *The Human Side of Enterprise*
C. Wright Mills's *The Sociological Imagination*

The Macat Library By Discipline

Thomas Piketty's *Capital in the Twenty-First Century*
Robert D. Putman's *Bowling Alone*
David Riesman's *The Lonely Crowd: A Study of the Changing American Character*
Edward Said's *Orientalism*
Joan Wallach Scott's *Gender and the Politics of History*
Theda Skocpol's *States and Social Revolutions*
Max Weber's *The Protestant Ethic and the Spirit of Capitalism*

THEOLOGY

Augustine's *Confessions*
Benedict's *Rule of St Benedict*
Gustavo Gutiérrez's *A Theology of Liberation*
Carole Hillenbrand's *The Crusades: Islamic Perspectives*
David Hume's *Dialogues Concerning Natural Religion*
Immanuel Kant's *Religion within the Boundaries of Mere Reason*
Ernst Kantorowicz's *The King's Two Bodies: A Study in Medieval Political Theology*
Søren Kierkegaard's *The Sickness Unto Death*
.C. S. Lewis's *The Abolition of Man*
Saba Mahmood's *The Politics of Piety: The Islamic Revival and the Feminist Subject*
Baruch Spinoza's *Ethics*
Keith Thomas's *Religion and the Decline of Magic*

Macat Disciplines

Access the greatest ideas and thinkers across entire disciplines, including

AFRICANA STUDIES

Chinua Achebe's *An Image of Africa: Racism in Conrad's Heart of Darkness*

W. E. B. Du Bois's *The Souls of Black Folk*

Zora Neale Hurston's *Characteristics of Negro Expression*

Martin Luther King Jr.'s *Why We Can't Wait*

Toni Morrison's *Playing in the Dark: Whiteness in the American Literary Imagination*

Macat analyses are available from all good bookshops and libraries.

Access hundreds of analyses through one, multimedia tool.

Join free for one month **library.macat.com**

Macat Disciplines

Access the greatest ideas and thinkers across entire disciplines, including

FEMINISM, GENDER AND QUEER STUDIES

Simone De Beauvoir's
The Second Sex

Michel Foucault's
History of Sexuality

Betty Friedan's
The Feminine Mystique

Saba Mahmood's
*The Politics of Piety:
The Islamic Revival and
the Feminist Subject*

Joan Wallach Scott's
*Gender and the
Politics of History*

Mary Wollstonecraft's
*A Vindication of the
Rights of Woman*

Virginia Woolf's
A Room of One's Own

Judith Butler's
Gender Trouble

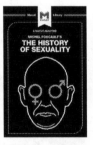

Macat Disciplines

Access the greatest ideas and thinkers across entire disciplines, including

Postcolonial Studies

Roland Barthes's *Mythologies*
Frantz Fanon's *Black Skin, White Masks*
Homi K. Bhabha's *The Location of Culture*
Gustavo Gutiérrez's *A Theology of Liberation*
Edward Said's *Orientalism*
Gayatri Chakravorty Spivak's *Can the Subaltern Speak?*

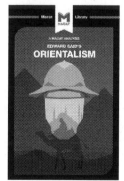

Macat analyses are available from all good bookshops and libraries.

Access hundreds of analyses through one, multimedia tool.
Join free for one month **library.macat.com**

Macat Pairs

Analyse historical and modern issues from opposite sides of an argument. Pairs include:

HOW TO RUN AN ECONOMY

John Maynard Keynes's
The General Theory OF Employment, Interest and Money

Classical economics suggests that market economies are self-correcting in times of recession or depression, and tend toward full employment and output. But English economist John Maynard Keynes disagrees.

In his ground-breaking 1936 study *The General Theory*, Keynes argues that traditional economics has misunderstood the causes of unemployment. Employment is not determined by the price of labor; it is directly linked to demand. Keynes believes market economies are by nature unstable, and so require government intervention. Spurred on by the social catastrophe of the Great Depression of the 1930s, he sets out to revolutionize the way the world thinks

Milton Friedman's
The Role of Monetary Policy

Friedman's 1968 paper changed the course of economic theory. In just 17 pages, he demolished existing theory and outlined an effective alternate monetary policy designed to secure 'high employment, stable prices and rapid growth.'

Friedman demonstrated that monetary policy plays a vital role in broader economic stability and argued that economists got their monetary policy wrong in the 1950s and 1960s by misunderstanding the relationship between inflation and unemployment. Previous generations of economists had believed that governments could permanently decrease unemployment by permitting inflation—and vice versa. Friedman's most original contribution was to show that this supposed trade-off is an illusion that only works in the short term.

Macat analyses are available from all good bookshops and libraries.

Access hundreds of analyses through one, multimedia tool.
Join free for one month **library.macat.com**

Macat Disciplines

Access the greatest ideas and thinkers across entire disciplines, including

TOTALITARIANISM

Sheila Fitzpatrick's, *Everyday Stalinism*
Ian Kershaw's, *The "Hitler Myth"*
Timothy Snyder's, *Bloodlands*

Macat Pairs

*Analyse historical and modern issues
from opposite sides of an argument.
Pairs include:*

INTERNATIONAL RELATIONS IN THE 21ST CENTURY

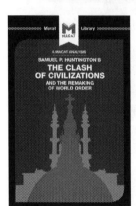

Samuel P. Huntington's
The Clash of Civilisations

In his highly influential 1996 book, Huntington offers a vision of a post-Cold War world in which conflict takes place not between competing ideologies but between cultures. The worst clash, he argues, will be between the Islamic world and the West: the West's arrogance and belief that its culture is a "gift" to the world will come into conflict with Islam's obstinacy and concern that its culture is under attack from a morally decadent "other."

Clash inspired much debate between different political schools of thought. But its greatest impact came in helping define American foreign policy in the wake of the 2001 terrorist attacks in New York and Washington.

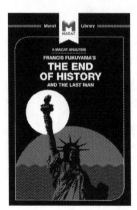

Francis Fukuyama's
The End of History and the Last Man

Published in 1992, *The End of History and the Last Man* argues that capitalist democracy is the final destination for all societies. Fukuyama believed democracy triumphed during the Cold War because it lacks the "fundamental contradictions" inherent in communism and satisfies our yearning for freedom and equality. Democracy therefore marks the endpoint in the evolution of ideology, and so the "end of history." There will still be "events," but no fundamental change in ideology.

Macat Disciplines

Access the greatest ideas and thinkers across entire disciplines, including

MAN AND THE ENVIRONMENT

 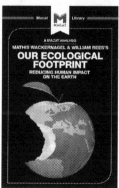

The Brundtland Report's, *Our Common Future*
Rachel Carson's, *Silent Spring*
James Lovelock's, *Gaia: A New Look at Life on Earth*
Mathis Wackernagel & William Rees's, *Our Ecological Footprint*

Macat analyses are available from all good bookshops and libraries.

Access hundreds of analyses through one, multimedia tool.
Join free for one month **library.macat.com**

Macat Pairs

Analyse historical and modern issues from opposite sides of an argument. Pairs include:

HOW WE RELATE TO EACH OTHER AND SOCIETY

Jean-Jacques Rousseau's
The Social Contract

Rousseau's famous work sets out the radical concept of the 'social contract': a give-and-take relationship between individual freedom and social order.

If people are free to do as they like, governed only by their own sense of justice, they are also vulnerable to chaos and violence. To avoid this, Rousseau proposes, they should agree to give up some freedom to benefit from the protection of social and political organization. But this deal is only just if societies are led by the collective needs and desires of the people, and able to control the private interests of individuals. For Rousseau, the only legitimate form of government is rule by the people.

Robert D. Putnam's
Bowling Alone

In *Bowling Alone*, Robert Putnam argues that Americans have become disconnected from one another and from the institutions of their common life, and investigates the consequences of this change.

Looking at a range of indicators, from membership in formal organizations to the number of invitations being extended to informal dinner parties, Putnam demonstrates that Americans are interacting less and creating less "social capital" – with potentially disastrous implications for their society.

It would be difficult to overstate the impact of *Bowling Alone*, one of the most frequently cited social science publications of the last half-century.